323

Food Combining

for

Spring Summer

Autumn Winter

ROUMIANKA LAZAROVA

SERIES "PROPERLY COMBINING OF FOOD"

323 Recipes
Food Combining for Spring Summer Autumn Winter

Copyrights

ISBN: 9781980693031

This Page Intentionally Left Blank

This page intentionally left blank

CONTENTS

This Page Intentionally Left Blank

ABOUT THE BOOK

Every member of our family strives to be healthy, energetic and complete, both at work and at school, and at home. Unfortunately, this is not always easy with a magic wand. We strive to achieve our healthy lifestyle by incorporating less of the generally accepted recommendations. Naturally, this begins with nutrition, walks, stress reduction, more emotions that are positive and enough sleep.

Because all we are predisposed to gaining weight, we are especially careful about nutrition issues. We tried different diets. It is quite difficult to reach a consensus on how to feed all together and to feel good. Because, believe me, it is very exhausting to cook different food for any according to taste and whim. A few years ago, we united our understanding. We began to eat by following the most general principles of separate eating. Of course, we do not fall into extremes, but we all feel great. Healthy, energetic and quite successful.

I decided to share a small portion of the recipes that we prepare for our meal according to the basic principles of food combining nutrition for a period of 1 month in the book: "Weight loss. 4 weeks meal plan to lose 17 lbs. Food combining recipes". This book enjoys a success.

The results really are impressive. The interest in the proposed menus is quite large. This provoked me and encouraged me to continue to share my experience of preparing homemade delicious food, of course, following the general principles of food combining. Now, the recipes are not for one month, but for each season, for the whole year. Almost every person sometimes happens to let go and then seek a way to be "on the track", again. That's why it's good to have the opportunity in all seasons to start something new or to go on with something good that we have forgotten

That's why I made this selection of 323 of my recipes for food combining in Spring, Summer, Autumn and Winter. For each season, suitable combinations for lunch and dinner are prepared. In some of the cases, the offer is for main dish and soup, main course and salad, soup and salad, etc. **The main menus are 220, of which 110 for lunch and 110 for dinner**. All recipes in this book are suitable not only for overweight people who want to lose weight, but also for all who want to change their diet, be healthy and energetic.

Each recipe complies with the principles of food combining. Each menu offered also takes into account the combination of both meals. The products incorporated in the recipes are the healthy quantities for four servings. You do not have to follow strictly any combination of dishes in the menus. You can only eat one of the meal in the menu offered. For example, only soup, only salad or just a dish. After each recipe, there is advice about what to eat or how to combine - "Serve with" or "Combines with".

You can comfortably make your combinations, but be careful to combine the products during one meal. Better eat one larger dish if you are very hungry, than start chaotically getting everything you have in the refrigerator or in the closet.

A WORD FROM THE AUTHOR

1. You cannot get lasting weight loss through starvation. This can be reached by proper, regular and complete nutrition

1.1. Mistakes we make before we think seriously about our health, physical and peace of mind and reinforcement:
   - We do not have breakfast on a regular basis, or have breakfast on the go, and without thinking about what we put in our mouths.
   - We do not find the right time for lunch.
   - A dinner ... ... what do we do when we get back from work? There is a complete chaos in our head and stomach. Firstly, we sit in front of the TV set. Naturally, we take something that is easiest to us: sandwiches, chips, ice cream, desserts, carbonated beverages, pizza, potatoes, chicken with rice, bread, and so on. Now this is already in our past.

1.2. Our healthy diet includes compulsory breakfast, lunch and dinner.
Breakfast. To help our metabolism work at a fast pace, to begin the regulation of our weight, we need to learn firstly to eat regularly. It is important to know that people who have breakfast have a better chance of losing weight than those who missed it. What breakfast we would choose depends on the energy we need during the day. The possibilities are many: eggs with vegetables; oat flakes with linseed; 2oz. raw nuts; green shake; vegetable smoothie or a single fruit. Each of these breakfast suggestions are great for people on a diet. For example, a small handful of cashew nuts or almonds will be enough to reduce your hunger, increase energy levels, and make your brain work better. I think it's worth trying. There is nothing more enjoyable than starting a day with a cup of hot coffee or tea, with breakfast that we may have prepared in the evenings. So we will save some of our morning stress.
Lunch - between 12 pm and 2 pm. Dinner - between 6 pm and

3

8 pm. If you wish, each of us can spend some time for lunch, and more for dinner with family or friends. In addition, when you are alone you can try to cook on the recipes from this book. You will find out how pleasant it is to cook listening your favorite music, preparing yourself a warm, aromatic and delicious dinner. You will feel like you relax after a hard, working day just that way.

2. *Why did I choose to feed on the food combining system?*
Even if you are not interested in weight reduction, there is no reason not to include the food combining in your life. This instantly reduces stress on digestive glands and actually improves the body's ability to eliminate waste and absorb nutrients.

If you have not yet chosen a specific system die and do not know how to get started, you can try the way my family has been eating for many years. This is the method of food combining. Maybe it sounds familiar to you, but you still have not had the chance to try it. What is the essence: In single meal do not mix foods which combination leads to problematic digestion and difficulties in absorbing nutrients. For this reason, it is best for a meal to consist of carefully selected products that are tolerated and assisted each other in the process of digestion. The purpose of combining foods is to ensure easy digestion, according to the specifics of the human digestive system.

Simply put, without going into scientific theories and terms, it is easiest to assume that the foods are at least three types: proteins, carbohydrates and neutral. The first two should never be mixed up, and the third one can be mixed with everything:

- Proteins are meat, fish, eggs, dairy products (some nutritionists even accept that different protein groups should not be mixed - for example: meat and cheese ...).
- Carbohydrates are bread and pasta (my great passion for pasta, but ...), pulses, rice, potatoes, corn.
- Neutral are vegetables, leafy vegetables and others.

What does this really mean? I forgot the sandwiches, pizzas, burrito, tacos, fried potatoes, meat with baked potatoes, fish with potato purée, chicken with rice, and so on. Now when I've learned to really think what to eat, I've found hundreds of combinations of meat, vegetables, fish, eggs, spices, aromas, and the pleasure of eating homemade food. I am in love with salads - I actually lost weight for the first time in the spring because I ate a huge amount of green salad in any combination. Most often, it was a fresh addition to a dish with chicken or fish. I began to feel more efficient. Acids and weight in my stomach disappeared. I rarely get sick and recover faster.

In addition to the three main meals, I allow myself a little dark chocolate or fruit (not more than 1 ounce at a time). Of course, they are consumed at least 2 hours after the main meal.

3. I follow a few simple, acceptable rules.
- I drink at least 8 - 10 glasses of water a day;
- No carbonated beverages;
- I do not consume white flour or products in which it is incorporated;
- I do not consume white sugar or artificial sweeteners;
- I do not consume large amounts of salt, just a pinch to the dish that has to be flavored with other fresh spices and those that speed up metabolism;
- I've forgotten about croissants, biscuits, pie, protein blocks, and so on.

When we have a celebration at home, I prepare some dainty of fruits, nuts, whole grain flour, and brown sugar. This, of course, is not every day, it happens rarely and impresses us and enjoys enough. So we are not quite isolated from the real taste of good things. However, they can be prepared very easily at home. Therefore, the choice of products we can use is very large.

4. Other actions that relieve my diet of a healthy life and nutrition.

- I use a few little tricks that help me not to deviate easily from my decision for a healthy lifestyle. I preliminary consider and compile a menu for the whole week. I prepare a list of the products I will need to prepare each of the planned meals. It is much easier when you go to the market. I try to keep it. Temptations and costs are less. The time elapsed for a market is also planned.

- The price. Everyone thinks that healthy food is much more expensive than ready-made frozen foods or otherwise prepared meals. This, of course, is not true. My experience shows the following. When using seasonal fruits and vegetables, fresh meat and fish when preparing homemade hot food there are two undisputed benefits for us. The first one is that homemade meals are always more useful if they are prepared using appropriate technology and the second one is - it is cheaper.

- It is not a problem to cook a few more meals in the evening. The next day you can have a homemade lunch, an afternoon snack, and why not a piece of chocolate.

The idea of all that I wrote down here is to eat good foods, but not to put them in our stomach at the same time. Let think about how to combine them so that we get the variety and full supply of the nutrients needed for our body: vitamins, minerals, enzymes, fiber, proteins, fats, carbohydrates, and so on.

5. How is prepared the food according to the recipes from this book?

- There are used products, meat, vegetables and herbs typical for each season: Spring, Summer, Autumn, Winter:

- There are used fresh meat, chicken and fish with no fat or skin, having in mind at what season they are most suitable for consumption;

- Healthy fats are included in each recipe: olive oil, vegetable oil, butter in small quantities;

- It is used a very small amount of salt and the other spices deliver the specific home-made flavor of every dish made during each season;

- Kitchen dishes (pans and pots) with non-stick bottom are used; - Cooking methods are stewing, cooking and baking in an oven or BBQ. Frying is not allowed.

6. How was composed the menu for each lunch or dinner, for each of the season.

Each dish is cooked, while respecting the principles of food combining. Were used products that are typical for each season and which can be combined with each other. The flavor of the food is supplemented by the use of various fresh spices or ground dried spices and roots. Recipes for soups or salads are also proposed, which are also combined with the ingredients in the main dish.

If the offer for dinner is from just one dish or soup, the quantity of portions is consistent with not exceeding the calories of the day. Under such a recipe, there are options on how to combine.

It is a good idea when choosing a meal plan for the whole day to choose a different menu for lunch and dinner. This will give your body a variety of different nutrients. I prefer to eat at lunch a carbohydrate meal (for example, potatoes), and for dinner, proteins (e.g. chicken or fish with vegetables). Sometimes, however, I break this rule. However, that is not a problem, because I am having dinner early and there's plenty of time for my stomach to cope with everything I had with dinner.

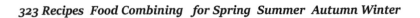

This page intentionally left blank

SPRING - LUNCH

1.1. SOUP OF MINCED LAMB MEAT

Ingredients for 4 servings:
- 11 oz. (312 g.) Ground Lamb
- 11 oz. (312 g.) fresh spinach
- 1 sweet onion
- 1 teaspoon butter

Spices: 1 teaspoon of ginger, anise 2 seeds, salt to taste.

Way of preparation:

Knead the Ground Lamb with the ginger, a little salt and the crushed anise. In order to make the mixture softer, add a little hot water. Make about 30 small balls. Smother the chopped spinach and onion in butter; add a little salt and a little water. In a saucepan with 4 cups of hot water drop one by one meat balls. Allow the soup to boil for 30 minutes. Put steamed spinach and onion. Serve the soup warm.

Optionally at serving can spice the soup with freshly squeezed lemon juice.

Serve with: *Spinach with Olives*

1.2. SPINACH WITH OLIVES

Ingredients for 4 servings:
- 26 oz. (740 g.) cooked, drained and chopped spinach
- 8 pitted black olives, sliced on rings
- 8 green olives
- 1 tablespoon sliced almonds
- 1 clove finely chopped garlic
- 2 tablespoons olive oil

Spices: ground coriander, ground nutmeg, salt to taste.

Way of preparation:

In a saucepan with non-stick coating heat the olive oil and fry for 1 minute the almonds together with the garlic. Add olives and fry

1 minute more. Then put the spinach and the spices. Cook for about 3 minutes. Serve meal warm.

2.1. CHICKEN WITH MUSHROOMS

Ingredients for 4 servings:
- ½ small Chicken
- 9 oz. (255 g.) mushrooms
- 2 tablespoons oil
- 1 sweet onion chopped
- 2 medium carrots, cut into rings
- ½ cup of white wine
- 2 cloves of garlic

Spices: 10 grains coriander, 2 seeds cardamom, 1 teaspoon dried thyme, juice of ½ lemon, 10 peppercorns, salt to taste.

Way of preparation:
Wash the chicken and place it in a saucepan with cold water. When the water begins to boil, add salt, reduce the heat and remove the foam. When the chicken is cooked, remove it from the saucepan, allow it to cool slightly. Bone the chicken, divide it into portions.

Heat the oil. Add the onions, the carrots, the mushrooms and garlic. Stir periodically. After 5 minutes, put the wine, all the spices and the chicken. After it boils, cover with a lid and leave to simmer for 10 minutes. Serve meal warm.

Serve with: *Baby Spinach Salad*

2.2. BABY SPINACH SALAD

Ingredients for 4 servings:
- 12 oz. (340g.) Baby Spinach
- 3 green onion
- 1 tablespoon walnuts
- 4 fresh radishes

Spices: 2 tablespoons finely chopped parsley, 2 tablespoons olive oil, vinegar or lemon juice, salt to taste.

Way of preparation:

Wash the spinach thoroughly with cold water. Cut it into thin strips. Add the finely chopped onion and ground walnuts. Season the salad with salt, olive oil and vinegar or lemon juice. Decorate with radishes.

3.1. CARROTS AND CELERY SOUP

Ingredients for 4 servings:

- 2 large carrots
- 3 green onions
- ¼ head of celery
- 2 teaspoons tomato paste
- 1 egg

Spices: 5-6 sprigs of dill, ground black pepper and salt to taste.

Way of preparation:

Clean, wash and finely chop the carrots, celery and onions and drop them to boil in 4 cups salted water until they soften. Shortly before removing the soup from the heat, add the tomato paste diluted in some hot water. To finish the soup - add a thickener with well beaten egg.

Serve the soup warm, season it with pepper and chopped dill.

Serve with: "Green" Eggs in The Oven

3.2. "GREEN" EGGS IN THE OVEN

Ingredients for 4 servings:

- 12 large eggs
- 2 tablespoons sunflower oil
- ½ cup finely chopped parsley
- ½ tablespoon basil

Spices: 1 teaspoon grated nutmeg 1 teaspoon ground coriander, ground black pepper and salt to taste.

Way of preparation:

Beat the eggs well with 1 teaspoon of salt. Add the basil, parsley and all the spices. Pour mixture into greased with sunflower oil, warmed pan. Sprinkle with sunflower oil and bake the dish in a moderately heated oven 392 F / 200 C. Bake for about 10 minutes. Serve the dish warm.

4.1. LAMB MEAT WITH TOMATOES

Ingredients for 4 servings:
- 1 lb. 6 oz. (624 g.) Lamb Meat
- 2 cloves of garlic
- 3 green onions
- 12 oz. (340 g.) Cherry Tomatoes
- 2 tablespoons sunflower oil

Spices: 2 tablespoons finely chopped parsley, 1 teaspoon paprika, 1 bay leaf, ground black pepper and salt to taste.

Way of preparation:
Cut the meat into portions and smother it with sunflower oil. After 10 minutes, add the garlic, onions, black pepper and salt. Pour 1 ½ cups of hot water. When the meat is almost cooked, add the tomatoes and bay leaf. Cook the dish over low heat until the meat is tender well.

Sprinkled with finely chopped parsley. Serve the dish warm with fresh salad.

Combines with:

Vegetable salads and vegetable soups - without potatoes; to them may be added meat, chicken, ham, mushrooms, olives (prepared according to the recipes of this book).

5.1. TURKY BREAST SOUP WITH VEGETABLES

Ingredients for 4 servings:
- 12 oz. (340 g.) Turkey Breast
- 2 medium carrots
- 1 sweet onion
- 2 ribs celery
- 2 tablespoons sunflower oil
- 3 mini sweet peppers (red, orange, yellow)

Spices: ¼ teaspoon oregano, lemon juice or vinegar, ground black pepper and salt to taste.

Way of preparation:
Wash the Turkey Breast and cut it into small pieces. Chop finely the onion, the carrots, the mini sweet peppers and the celery. Put the Turkey Breast on fire with 4 ½ cups of cold water. When it starts to boil, reduce heat and keep removing the foam. When the meat is almost cooked, add 1 tablespoons sunflower oil, the vegetables, salt and ground black pepper. Allow the soup to simmer for 20 minutes. Before removing it from the heat and add the oregano.
Season the soup with lemon juice or vinegar. Serve the soup warm with fresh salad.

Combines with:
Vegetable salads and vegetable dishes - without potatoes; to them may be added meat, chicken, ham, mushrooms, olives (prepared according to the recipes of this book).

6.1. TROUT FILLETS WITH FENNEL BAKED IN OVEN

Ingredients for 4 servings:
- 1 lb.12 oz. (800 g.) Fresh Steelhead Trout Fillets
- Juice of 1 lemon
- 1 yellow onion
- ½ head fennel
- 2 cloves of garlic
- 2 tablespoons sunflower oil

- 1 tablespoon tomato paste

Spices: 2 bay leaves, 2 grains allspice, 1 lemon, 2 tablespoons finely chopped parsley, ground black pepper and salt to taste.

Way of preparation:

Sprinkle the fish fillets with lemon juice, salt and ground black. Let them stand for 1 hour. Cut the onion and fennel into slices and smother them hot oil. Add salt, black pepper, the finely chopped garlic, the tomato paste dissolved in a little cold water, bay leaf and allspice. Pour 1 cup of hot water, cook for 10 minutes on medium heat. Pour mixture into a baking dish. Sprinkle it with freshly cut parsley. Arrange the fish fillets on top. Cover fish with lemon sliced on rings. Roast the dish in a moderately high heat 392 F / 200 C, until it remains on fat (about 30 minutes).

The ready dish can be served hot.

Serve with: *Salad of Carrots and Fish Caviar*

6.2. SALAD OF CARROTS AND FISH CAVIAR

Ingredients for 4 servings:

- 4 medium fresh carrots
- 4 tablespoons fish caviar
- ¼ head of celery
- 12 olives

Spices: 1 tablespoon olive oil, 2 tablespoons lemon juice, 1 tablespoon dill, salt to taste.

Way of preparation:

Wash and grate the carrots and celery on fine grater. Put them in a bowl, add the dill and the salt. Pour over with the olive oil and lemon juice.

Decorate the salad with olives and a sprig of parsley. Add 1 tablespoon of fish caviar to each serving of salad.

7.1. SOUP OF VEAL SHANK

Ingredients for 4 servings:

- 1 lb.10 oz. (740 g.) Veal Shank with bone
- 2 medium carrots
- ¼ head celery

Spices: 2 tablespoons finely chopped parsley, 1 tablespoon grated horseradish, 5 tablespoons of vinegar, ground black pepper and salt to taste.

Way of preparation:

Pour over the shank with 6 cups cold water. Put it on high heat until boil. Reduce the heat and keep removing the foam. When the meat is almost cooked, remove the shank and remove the meat from the bones. Cut the meat into larger pieces and return to the boiling water. Add the sliced carrots and celery, the salt and the pepper. Allow the soup to simmer for 20 minutes. Serve the soup hot, sprinkled with chopped parsley.

In a small bowl mix the grated horseradish, season it with vinegar and salt. By choice anyone can add to their portion of this aromatic and spicy mixture.

<u>**Serve with:**</u> *Motley Salad with Ham*

7. 2.MOTLEY SALAD WITH HAM

Ingredients for 4 servings:

- 5 oz. (150 g.) Cooked Ham
- 1 smaller Cos Lettuce
- 1 smaller Red Oak Leaf Lettuce
- 1 small red onion
- 1 cup marinated mushrooms

Spices: 2 tablespoons olive oil, 2 tablespoons cider apple vinegar, black pepper and salt to taste.

Way of preparation:

Shred the leaves of lettuce. Cut the red onion and the ham into thin strips. Drain the mushrooms from the marinade. Put the ingredients in a salad bowl. Add salt and mix gently.

Pour over the salad with olive oil and vinegar, sprinkle with pepper. Serve salad immediately.

8.1. LAMB SOUP WITH SPINACH

Ingredients for 4 servings:
- 10 oz. (285 g.) Lamb Meat
- 7 oz. (200 g.) fresh spinach
- 3 green onion
- 2 green garlic
- 1 teaspoon of butter
- 2 teaspoons tomato paste

Spices: 1 teaspoon paprika, a few spearmint leaves, 6 sprigs of dill, ground black pepper and salt to taste.

Way of preparation:
Wash the lamb meat and cut it into small pieces. Put it on fire with 5-6 cups of cold water. When it starts to boil, reduce the heat and keep removing the foam. When the meat is almost cooked, add the onion, the garlic, the chopped spinach, the tomato paste, salt, the red pepper. Allow the soup to simmer for 15 minutes.
Before removing it from the heat, add the butter, black pepper, the chopped spearmint and dill.
Serve the soup hot.
Serve with: *Lamb with Lemon*

8.2. LAMB WITH LEMON

Ingredients for 4 servings:
- 1 lb. 8 oz. (680 g.) Lamb Meat
- 2 tablespoons oil

Spices: 1 teaspoon saffron, ¼ teaspoon of cinnamon and 1 lemon.

Way of preparation:
Put to boil olive oil, 1 ½ cup of water, saffron, cinnamon and the chopped lemon. When the mixture boils, add the chopped portions of lamb. Cook the dish on low heat until the meat becomes soft. Serve the meal warm.

9.1. SOUP OF FRESH MUSHROOMS AND POTATOES

Ingredients for 4 servings:
- 5 oz. (142 g.) Fresh Field Mushrooms
- 11 oz. (312 g.) white potatoes
- 3 green onions
- 1 medium carrot
- ½ teaspoon butter

Spices: 1 bay leaf, lemon juice, 2 tablespoons finely chopped parsley, 1 tablespoon finely chopped parsley dill, ground black pepper and salt to taste.

Way of preparation:
Clean, wash and chop the mushrooms into slices. Cut the carrots and onion into thin rings. Put together the mushrooms and carrots to be boiled in 4 cups salted water. After 5 minutes, add the potatoes cut into small cubes and bay leaf. When the potatoes are tender add the butter and green onion. Serve the soup warm with lemon juice. Sprinkle it with ground black pepper, chopped dill and parsley.

Serve with: Spinach "Meatballs"

9.2. SPINACH "MEATBALLS"

Ingredients for 4 servings:
- 1 lb. (454g.) Fresh Spinach
- 12 oz. (340 g.) boiled potatoes
- 3 green onions
- 1 teaspoon butter
- 2 tablespoons sunflower oil

Spices: 1 tablespoon spearmint leaves, 2 tablespoons finely chopped parsley, ground black pepper and salt to taste.

Way of preparation:
Clean, wash, chop, chop the spinach. Smother it with a the butter. Add cooked and pureed potatoes, the finely chopped onion, the pepper, the salt, the spearmint and the parsley. Knead the mixture. Shape meatballs from and time to time oiling your

hands. Roll the meatballs. Arrange them in a heated, oiled pan. Put to bake in a preheated oven at 392 F / 200 C. Sprinkle them with oil and bake 20 minutes. Serve warm with green salad.

10.1. BAKED MACKEREL WITH ALMONDS

Ingredients for 4 servings:
- 3 lbs. (1.360 g.) Fresh Fish - Mackerel
- 3 tablespoons lemon juice
- 2 tablespoons oil
- 1 tablespoon peeled almonds
- 11 oz. (312 g.) tomatoes

Spices: ground black pepper and salt to taste.

Way of preparation:

Clean and wash the fish. With a sharp knife make a small diagonal cuts and rub with salt and pepper. Put the fish in a baking dish, pour with lemon juice and then bake in a preheated moderately high at 392 F / 200 C.

Separately, smother with a little oil the chopped almonds. Remove them from the pan and in the same oil smother the chopped tomatoes. Boil it until a thick sauce. Season it with salt and pepper. Put the baked fish in a heated dish. Sprinkle with almonds. Just before serving pour with the prepared tomato sauce.

Combines with:

Vegetable salads and vegetable soups - without potatoes; to them may be added fish, seafood, mushrooms, olives (prepared according to the recipes of this book).

11.1. SPICY LAMB STEW

Ingredients for 4 servings:
- 27 oz. (765 g.) Lamb Meat
- 3 tablespoons of sunflower oil
- 2 jalapeno peppers

- 1 sweet onion
- 1 cup of fresh mushrooms
- 3 mini sweet red peppers
- 3 roma tomatoes
- 2 cloves of garlic

Spices: ½ teaspoon savory, 2 teaspoons paprika, ½ bunch of dill, 2 tablespoons finely chopped parsley, salt to taste.

Way of preparation:

Cut the lamb into small pieces; smother it with chopped onion and oil. Add the paprika and 1 cup of hot water. Continue to smother, with chopped mini sweet red peppers. When the meat becomes soft, add the tomatoes, garlic cloves, cut into julienne mushrooms, jalapeno peppers as whole and salt. Cook the dish on low heat 15-20 minutes. Remove the dish from the heat and add the finely chopped savory, parsley and dill.

Combines with:

Vegetable salads and vegetable soups - without potatoes; to them may be added meat, chicken, ham, mushrooms, olives (prepared according to the recipes of this book).

12.1. COTTAGE ROAST WHOLE CHICKEN

Ingredients for 4 servings:

- 1 Small Whole Chicken
- 1 cup petite diced tomatoes
- 2 red sweet peppers
- 6 green onions
- 2 garlic cloves
- 2 tablespoons of sunflower oil

Spices: 10 spearmint leaves, 2 tablespoons finely chopped parsley, ground black pepper and salt to taste.

Way of preparation:

Sprinkle the chicken with salt and pepper. Smear it with sunflower oil and put it in a tray. Around him allocate the chopped onions, garlic, peppers, tomatoes, spearmint. Add salt and remaining sunflower oil. Stir the mixture, add 1 cup of hot water and put to roast in a moderately heated oven 374 F / 190 C, about 1 hour.

Serve the chicken warm. Garnish with a part of the roasted vegetables, sprinkled with parsley.

Combines with:

Vegetable salads and vegetable soups - without potatoes; to them may be added meat, chicken, ham, mushrooms, olives (prepared according to the recipes of this book).

13.1. FISH SOUP WITH CURCUMA

Ingredients for 4 servings:
- 12 oz. (340 g.) Tilapia Fillets
- 2 tablespoons sunflower oil
- 5 green onions
- 2 cloves of crushed garlic
- 1 teaspoon curcuma (turmeric powder)
- 1 teaspoon of grated ginger

Spices: 2 tablespoons lemon juice, 2 tablespoons finely chopped parsley, ground black pepper and salt to taste.

Way of preparation:

Heat the oil and sauté the fillets of fish with the chopped onions, garlic, grated ginger and curcuma for 5 minutes. Add the salt, the ground black pepper and 4 cups of hot water. Simmer for 10 – 15 minutes. Season the soup with lemon juice and sprinkle with chopped parsley.

Serve with: *Braised Carrots with Onions*

13.2. BRAISED CARROTS WITH ONION

Ingredients for 4 servings:
- ✓ 22 oz. (624 g.) carrots
- ✓ 2 white large onions
- ✓ 1 teaspoon butter

Spices: 1 clove, 1 tablespoon finely chopped dill, ground black pepper and salt to taste.

Way of preparation:

Clean and chop the carrots into slices and onion into quarters. Smother them in butter, add spices, reduce heat and smother another 10-15 minutes with a little water. Sprinkle with chopped dill.

14.1. GREEN ONION SOUP

Ingredients for 4 servings:
- 9 oz. (255 g.) Green Onions
- ½ cup fennel, cut into thin strips
- ¼ cup white wine
- 1 tablespoon sunflower oil

Spices: 2 tablespoons finely chopped of parsley, ground black pepper and salt to taste.

Way of preparation:

Clean, wash and cut into large onion. Smother it and the fennel in oil. After 10 minutes add the wine. Pour 3 cups hot water, ground black pepper and salt to taste.

Season finished soup with chopped parsley and serve it warm.

Serve with: *Potatoes with Garlic Baked in an Oven*

14.2. POTATOES WITH GARLIC BAKED IN AN OVEN

Ingredients for 4 servings:
- 1 lb. 10 oz. (737 g.) Russet Potatoes
- 2 teaspoons butter
- 3 cloves of garlic

Spices: 1 teaspoon paprika, ground black pepper and salt to taste.

Way of preparation:

Peel the potatoes, wash them and cut them into cubes. Drop them in boiling salted water for 10 minutes. Then drain them. Pour them into the pan. Sprinkle with paprika, ground black pepper, pressed garlic and melted butter. Bake potatoes in heated oven 410 F / 210 C, until golden brown. Serve them hot.

15.1. FRIED POACHED EGGS ON SPINACH PUREE

Ingredients for 4 servings:
- 12 large eggs
- 3 tablespoons sunflower oil
- 19.5 oz. (552 g.) fresh spinach
- 3 green onions
- 2 green garlic
- 1 teaspoon butter

Spices: 1 teaspoon paprika, ground black pepper and salt to taste.

Way of preparation:
Chop the spinach, green onions and green garlic finely. Smother them with butter. Add ground pepper and salt, blend. Pour the puree on the plate. On it, in every dish put 3 fried poached eggs. Sprinkle with paprika.

Combines with:
Vegetable salads and vegetable soups - without potatoes; to them may be added eggs, mushrooms, olives (prepared according to the recipes of this book).

16.1. LAMB SOUP WITH GINGER

Ingredients for 4 servings:
- 11oz. (312 g.) Lamb Meat
- 1 large carrot
- 3 green onions
- ¼ cup crisp celery
- 1 tablespoon sunflower oil
- 1 teaspoon tomato paste
- 2 cloves of garlic
- 1 teaspoon grated ginger

Spices: 1 coffee spoon cumin, 7-8 sprigs of parsley, ground black pepper and salt to taste.

Way of preparation:

Smother the chopped into small pieces meat in the oil. After 6-7 minutes, add the chopped ginger, onion, garlic, carrots and celery. Add the salt, the cumin, the pepper and the dissolved in a little warm water tomato paste. Mix well. After 5-6 minutes, pour over the mixture with 5 cups of hot water. Simmer the soup until the meat is tender altogether.

Serve the soup hot, sprinkled with chopped parsley.

Serve with: *Turkey Breasts Meatballs with Spinach*

16.2. TURKEY BREASTS MEATBALLS WITH SPINACH

Ingredients for 4 servings:

- 17 oz. (480 g.) Ground Turkey Breasts
- 5 oz. (142 g.) fresh spinach
- 3 green onions
- 3 tablespoons of sunflower oil

Spices: 3 tablespoons chopped parsley, 1 teaspoon paprika, ground black pepper and salt to taste.

Way of preparation:

Chop the onion finely and spinach. Smother them in oil. After add the Ground Turkey Breasts, chopped parsley, paprika, ground black pepper and salt to taste. Knead the mixture. While kneading the mince constantly re-oil your hands. Shape meatballs and arrange them in a heated pan greased with oil. Sprinkle the top with oil and put to roast in a preheated oven to 390 F / 200 C, for about 20 - 30 minutes. Serve them warm with a butter head salad.

17.1. TILAPIA FILLETS WITH VEGETABLES IN OVEN

Ingredients for 4 servings:

- 22 oz. (624 g.) Tilapia Fillets
- 4 oz.(113 g.) fresh mushrooms
- 2 small carrots

- ¼ cup crisp celery
- 3 - 4 green onions
- ½ cup petite diced tomatoes
- 10-12 olives
- 2 tablespoons of sunflower oil

Spices: 1 teaspoon paprika, 1 teaspoon oregano, ground black pepper and salt to taste.

Way of preparation:

Clean, wash and dice the carrots, the celery and the onion. Get them to smother with oil, 1 cupful of warm water and salt. Add the red pepper, cut into slices mushrooms, tomatoes and finally olives. Pour some hot water and add pepper and oregano. Leave the sauce to boil over low heat about 10-15 minutes, and then pour it into a baking dish. Arrange the fish on top. Bake the dish in a moderately heated oven for 392 F / 200 C, about 20 minutes. Serve the fish dish warm.

Combines with:

Vegetable salads and vegetable soups - without potatoes; to them may be added fish, seafood, fish caviar, mushrooms, olives (prepared according to the recipes of this book).

18.1. BROWN MUSHROOM SOUP WITH RICE

Ingredients for 4 servings:

- 5 oz. (142 g.) Brown Mushrooms
- 3 green onions
- 1 medium carrot
- ¼ cup crisp celery
- ¼ tablespoon butter
- 1/3 cup rice

Spices: 7 sprigs of dill, 3 tablespoon lemon juice, ground black pepper and salt to taste.

Way of preparation:

Clean and chop the mushrooms into slices. Cut the onions, celery and carrots into small cubes. Put together the mushrooms, celery, onion and carrots to boil in 4 cups salted water. Allow the soup to boil for about 10 minutes. Then pour the cleaned and washed rice. Simmer the soup for additional 15-20 minutes. Before removing it from the heat, put butter in it. Before presenting, season the soup with chopped dill, black pepper and freshly squeezed lemon juice.

Serve with: *Spinach with Rice*

18.2. SPINACH WITH RICE

Ingredients for 4 servings:
- 1 lb. (454 g.) Fresh Spinach
- 1 cup rice
- 1 yellow onion
- ½ cup diced tomatoes
- 3 tablespoons of sunflower oil

Spices: 1 tablespoon spearmint, 10 sprigs of parsley, ground black pepper and salt to taste.

Way of preparation:
Clean, wash and finely chop the spinach and the onion. Smother them in the oil for about 10 minutes, and then add the rice. Pour over the smothered mixture with 2-3 cups of hot water; add the black pepper, the spearmint, the finely chopped parsley and salt. Transfer the mixture into a baking dish. Arrange the sliced tomatoes on top and bake in preheated to 392 F / 200 C, oven until the water has evaporated and the rice is cooked.

19.1. LENTILS STEW

Ingredients for 4 servings:
- 2 cups cooked lentils
- 1 medium carrot
- ½ cup diced celery
- 1 small onion
- 4 cloves of garlic

- 2 tablespoons of sunflower oil

Spices: 2 teaspoons paprika, 10 sprigs parsley, salt to taste.

Way of preparation:

Heat the oil. Add the finely chopped carrot, the celery, the onion and the garlic. Stir and leave on the hot plate for 6 minutes. Then add the paprika, stir. Add 1 cup of hot water and let the mixture 15 minutes to boil. Add lentils - after 3 minutes the dish is ready. Add the finely chopped parsley. Serve the dish with fresh salad. The dish can be served both hot and cold.

Combines with:

Vegetable salads and vegetable soups - without potatoes; to them may be added pulses, mushrooms, olives, lentils, beans (prepared according to the recipes of this book).

20.1. CHICKEN QUARTERS WITH FRESH CABBAGE

Ingredients for 4 servings:

- 28 oz. (794 g.) Chicken Quarters
- 1 small fresh cabbage
- 3 tablespoon oil
- 2 jalapeno peppers

Spices: 3 tablespoons chopped parsley, 2 teaspoons paprika, ground black pepper and salt to taste.

Way of preparation:

Wash the chicken quarters. Sprinkle with oil, salt, paprika and pepper. Cut the cabbage into thin strips. Put it in a tray. Put the chicken quarters on the cabbage, whole jalapeno peppers, 1 teaspoon paprika, salt to taste and 1 cup hot water. Cover the pot with aluminum foil. Roast about 60 minutes at 392 F / 200 C. Allow to rest 10 minutes. Serve the dish warm, sprinkled with chopped parsley.

Combines with:

Vegetable salads and vegetable soups - without potatoes; to them may be added meat, chicken, ham, mushrooms, olives (prepared according to the recipes of this book).

21.1. BBQ: LAMB LOIN CHOPS

Ingredients for 4 servings:
- 8 Lamb Loin Chops
- 2 cloves of garlic
- 1 teaspoon rosemary
- ½ cup white wine
- 3 tablespoons sunflower oil

Spices: ground black pepper and salt to taste.

Way of preparation:

Roll lamb chops in crushed garlic and rosemary. Put them in a shallow baking dish. Pour them with white wine and sunflower oil. Let them stay in the cold marinade at least 2 hours. Remove lamb chops from marinade. Sprinkle them with salt and pepper. Bake the meat on a preheated grill. Flip them a few times - so they become juicy. Spray them with the marinade after each turn. Serve roll lamb chops warm with fresh vegetable salad.

Combines with:

Vegetable salads and vegetable soups - without potatoes; to them may be added meat, chicken, ham, mushrooms, olives (prepared according to the recipes of this book).

22.1. SCRAMBLED EGGS WITH GARLIC

Ingredients for 4 servings:
- 12 large eggs
- 4 green garlic or 4 cloves of garlic
- 2 cups fresh spinach
- 4 green onions
- 2 tablespoons sunflower oil

Spices: 1 teaspoon paprika, salt to taste.

Way of preparation:
Clean, wash and finely chop the onion and the garlic. Smother them with the fresh spinach, oil and salt to taste. Add the paprika and beaten eggs. Stirring until eggs whites become solid. Serve the dish warm.

<u>**Combines with:**</u>
Vegetable salads and vegetable soups - without potatoes; to them may be added eggs, mushrooms, olives (prepared according to the recipes of this book).

23.1. MUSSELS WITH WHITE WINE

Ingredients for 4 servings:
- 3 lbs. (1.360 g.) mussels with black shell
- 1 sweet onion
- 2 cloves of garlic
- 1 cup white wine
- 2 tablespoons of olive oil

Spices: ground black pepper and salt to taste.

Way of preparation:
In a deep saucepan place the washed and cleaned mussels. Add the chopped onion and garlic, white wine and pepper. Pour 1 cup of hot water. Put the lid on the pan. Cook the mussels 10 minutes until all the shells become open. Serve mussels immediately, while warm.

<u>**Serve with**</u>: *Salad of Fresh Onion with Anchovies*

23.2. SALAD OF GREEN ONION WITH ANCHOVIES

Ingredients for 4 servings:
- 6 oz. (170 g.) green onions
- 3 oz. (85g.) anchovies
- 8 olive
- 2 tablespoons olive or vegetable oil

Spices: 2 tablespoon lemon juice.

Way of preparation:
Clean, wash and finely chop the onion. Place it in a suitable plateau. Arrange the fish on the onion. Garnish with olives. Pour the salad with olive oil and lemon juice.

24.1. FRESH POTATOES WITH DILL

Ingredients for 4 servings:
- 2 lbs. 6 oz. (1.077 g.) fresh white potatoes
- 1 tablespoon butter
- 4 tablespoons potato flour

Spices: 3 tablespoons chopped dill, 2 tablespoons vinegar, ground black pepper and salt to taste.

Way of preparation:
Peel, wash and cut the potatoes into pieces. Boil them in salted water until soft. Fry the flour with the butter until golden. Add the water in which the potatoes were boiled, stirring continuously until you get thick porridge. Add the finely chopped dill and cook 5 minutes. Remove the sauce from heat and add the vinegar and the pepper. Pour the potatoes with this sauce and put back on the fire for a few minutes. Serve the dish warm.

Serve with: *Salad of Carrots and Red Onion*

24.2. SALAD OF CARROTS AND RED ONION

Ingredients for 4 servings:
- 1 Bunch Carrots
- 1 Bunch Beets
- 1 red onion
- 2 tablespoons olive oil

Spices: 2 - 3 tablespoons lemon juice, ground black pepper and salt to taste.

Way of preparation:
Grate the carrots, beets, onion on a medium grater. Add salt and ground black pepper to taste, the olive oil and the lemon juice. Stir the salad carefully.

25.1. LAMB MEAT ROASTED IN AN OVEN

Ingredients for 4 servings:
- 2 lbs. (907 g.) Lamb Meat
- 3 tablespoon oil
- 2 large sweet onions
- 3 large carrots, cut into rings

Spices: 2 cloves, 2 garlic cloves, 2 bay leaves, 1 teaspoon of thyme, ground black pepper and salt to taste.

Way of preparation:
Place the bottom of the tray chopped carrots, onions and all spices. Place the lamb meat on the mixture, pour it with olive oil. Cover the tray with a foil. Place the tray in a hot oven 356 F / 180 C . Roast the dish at 2 hours. Remove the foil and bake for 10 minutes - until the meat has browned. Serve each portion of roast meat with butter head salad.

Combines with:
Vegetable salads and vegetable soups - without potatoes; to them may be added meat, chicken, ham, mushrooms, olives (prepared according to the recipes of this book).

26.1. CHICKEN SOUP WITH FRESH MUSHROOMS

Ingredients for 4 servings:
- 11 oz. (312 g.) Fajita Chicken Meat
- 6 oz. (170 g.) Brown Sliced Mushrooms
- 1 sweet onion
- 1 teaspoon butter

Spices: 1 bay leaf, 1 bunch of dill, lemon juice, ground black pepper and salt to taste.

Way of preparation:
Finely chop the onion. Smother sliced mushrooms and onion with the butter. Sprinkle with pepper and salt. Add chicken cut into small pieces. Mix and after 3 - 5 minutes pour over the mixture with 4 cups of hot water. Add the bay leaves and let the soup to simmer 15-20 minutes.

Sprinkle each serving with chopped dill. Optionally, season the soup with lemon juice.

Serve with: *Vegetarian Stew*

26.2. VEGETARIAN STEW

Ingredients for 4 servings:
- 2 large carrots
- 1 cup celery, cut into thin strips
- 3 small zucchini
- 1 yellow onion
- 5 green onions
- 2 cloves of garlic
- 2 tablespoons sunflower oil

Spices: 2 bay leaves, 1 teaspoon paprika, ½ tablespoon vinegar, salt to taste

Way of preparation:
Clean, wash and cut the carrots, onion and zucchini into thin circles. Smother them in hot oil for 6 minutes. Add the chopped green onion, celery and paprika. Stir and place the bay leaves and the peeled garlic cloves. Add 1 cup water. When the water is boiled

away add the vinegar and close the saucepan tightly. Smother further 20 minutes.

27.1. LAMB SOUP

Ingredients for 4 servings:
- 11 oz. (312 g.) Lamb Meat
- 3 green onion
- 2 cloves of garlic
- 1 large carrot
- ½ cup diced celery
- 5 cherry tomatoes
- 2 tablespoons of oil

Spices: 1 teaspoon paprika, 10 spearmint leaves, 1 teaspoon savory, 3 tablespoon lemon juice, ground black pepper and salt to taste.

Way of preparation:
Wash the lamb meat and cut it into small pieces. Put it on the fire, cook it in the oil. When the meat starts change its color, add 5-6 cups of hot water. When the meat is almost cooked, add the chopped onion, garlic, carrots and celery. Add paprika, ground black pepper and salt to taste. Allow the soup to simmer for 20 minutes. Add whole cherry tomatoes

Before removing it from the heat, add whole cherry tomatoes, spearmint and savory.

When serving, season the soup with freshly squeezed lemon juice.

<u>Combines with:</u>

Vegetable salads and vegetable dishes - without potatoes; to them may be added meat, chicken, ham, mushrooms, olives (prepared according to the recipes of this book).

28.1. HERRING WITH WHITE WINE AND LEMON

Ingredients for 4 servings:
- 2 lbs. 4 oz. (1.020 g.) Herring (or other fish)
- 2 cloves of garlic
- 2 tablespoons of sunflower oil
- ½ cup white wine
- 2 tablespoons tomato sauce
- 1 lemon

Spices: 2 tablespoons of finely chopped parsley and salt to taste.

Way of preparation:
Wash the fishes. Salt them lightly and put them in an oiled baking dish. Cut the garlic into slices, mix it with the tomato sauce, parsley, white wine and oil. Pour over the fish with the mixture. Bake in a moderately heated oven 392 F / 200 C. When serving - decorate each fish with lemon slices.

<u>Combines with:</u>

Vegetable salads and vegetable soups - without potatoes; to them may be added fish, seafood, fish caviar, mushrooms, olives (prepared according to the recipes of this book).

29.1. STUFFED CHAMPIGNONS

Ingredients for 4 servings:
- 1 lb.10 oz. (737 g.) Fresh Large White Mushrooms
- juice of ½ lemons
- 4 green onion
- ½ tablespoon butter
- 3 tablespoons Grated Parmesan Cheese

Spices: 7-8 sprigs of dill, ground black pepper and salt to taste.

Way of preparation:
Clean the mushrooms well and rub them with lemon juice to not tarnish. Take little stumps, cut them retail and smother them in butter with chopped onion. Season the mixture with pepper and the finely chopped dill. Mix well and salt the mixture carefully. Caps Arrange mushrooms in a buttered baking dish. Fill them

with stewed mixture, sprinkle with Parmesan cheese. Bake in a moderately hot oven 390 F / 200 C , for about 10-15 minutes. Serve the mushrooms warm, garnish with an Iceberg Lettuce.
Serve with: *Spinach Puree with Mozzarella*

29.2. SPINACH PUREE WITH MOZZARELA

Ingredients for 4 servings:
- 1 lb. (454 g.) Fresh Spinach
- 1 teaspoon butter
- 2 cloves of garlic
- 5 oz. (142 g.) Shredded Mozzarella Cheese

Spices: ground black pepper and salt to taste.

Way of preparation:

Clean, wash, chop finely and smother the spinach with the butter and salt without adding water. Once tender, puree and add shredded mozzarella. Season it with ground black pepper and crushed garlic.

30.1. BBQ - CHICKEN WITH HERBS

Ingredients for 4 servings:
- 1 small chicken

For the marinade: ½ cup white wine, 1 tablespoon of tomato sauce, 2-3 tablespoons of oil, juice of ½ lemon, 1 grated onion, 2 cloves of crushed garlic, ½ teaspoon thyme, ½ teaspoon oregano, ½ teaspoon rosemary.

Way of preparation:

Cut the chicken in two halves in length. Prepare a marinade of all products. Mix them well. Put the chicken in a deep bowl and pour the marinade. Leave to stand for 2-3 hours in the refrigerator. Then drain. Roast it on the grill, 30 – 40 minutes. Serve each portion of grilled chicken with fresh vegetable salad.

You can bake it in the oven, also. During the roasting the meat shall be poured with remaining marinade.

<u>**Combines with:**</u>
Vegetable salads and vegetable soups - without potatoes; to them may be added meat, chicken, ham, mushrooms, olives (prepared according to the recipes of this book).

SPRING - DINNER

31.1. HALIBUT BAKED WITH WALNUTS

Ingredients for 4 servings:
- 1 lb. 12 oz. (800 g.) Halibut Fillets
- 3 yellow onions
- 2 cloves of garlic
- 1 tablespoon tomato paste
- 2 tablespoons of sunflower oil
- 2 tablespoons ground walnuts
- 1 lemon, cut into slices

Spices: 2 tablespoons chopped parsley, ground black pepper and salt to taste.

Way of preparation:
Wash the fish. Salt the fish, sprinkle with black pepper and let it stand for ¼ hour.
Cut the onion into slices and smother in oil. Salt and add the finely chopped garlic and tomato paste. When the onions soften pour ½ cup of hot water. Simmer the sauce for 3-4 minutes. Add the walnuts. Put the fish in a baking dish greased with oil. Pour with the walnuts mixture. On top arrange lemon slices and sprinkle with parsley. Bake the dish in a moderately hot oven
392 F / 200 C, until it remains on fat (for about 20 -30 minutes).
<u>**Serve with:**</u> *Salad with Tuna*

31.2. SALAD WITH TUNA

Ingredients for 4 servings:
- 1 Iceberg lettuce

- 4 oz. (110 g.) can of tuna
- 3 green onions
- 8 black olives

Spices: 2 tablespoons olive oil, 3 tablespoons lemon juice lemon, salt to taste.

Way of preparation:

Clean, wash and finely chop the lettuce and onion. Mix gently. Put the salad on a plate, top allocate small pieces tuna. Season it with salt, olive oil and lemon juice.

Decorate with olives and serve the salad cold.

32.1. LAMB MEAT WITH GREEN ONION

Ingredients for 4 servings:

- 1 lb. 10 oz. (737 g.) Lamb Meat
- 5 oz. (142 g.) green onions
- ¼ tablespoon butter
- 2 tablespoons chopped tomatoes

Spices: 10 sprigs of parsley, 1 teaspoon rosemary, ground black pepper and salt to taste.

Way of preparation:

Cut the lamb meat on pieces and pour it with 1 ½ cups of cold water. Once the water boils, reduce heat and remove the foam. After 30 minutes, add the tomatoes, the onion, the butter, the pepper and the salt. Stew on low heat until the meal remains on fat. When the dish is ready, add rosemary and parsley. Serve the dish warm.

Serve with: Spring Salad

32.2. SPRING SALAD

Ingredients for 4 servings:

- 1 Iceberg Lettuce

- 4 green onions
- 8 radishes

Spices: 2 tablespoons olive oil, finely chopped parsley, 4 slices of lemon, salt to taste.

Way of preparation:

Cut on large pieces cleaned and washed salad and onions. Add the finely chopped parsley and the radishes sliced into rings. Sprinkle with olive oil. Add salt in the salad just before serving.

Decorate the salad with lemon slices.

33.1. VEGETABLE RAGOUT

Ingredients for 4 servings:

- 2 lbs. (907 g.) White Potatoes
- 2 medium carrots
- 5 oz. (142 g.) small fresh white mushrooms
- 1 sweet onion
- 2 cloves of garlic
- 2 tablespoons sunflower oil

Spices: 6 mint leaves, 10 sprigs parsley, ground black pepper and salt to taste.

Way of preparation:

Heat the oil and smother the finely chopped onion. When it softened, add the peeled garlic cloves and the finely chopped carrots. Add ½ cup of water and smother the mixture for 10 minutes. Add the mushrooms and peeled and diced potatoes. Add 1 cup of hot water and cook the dish on low heat. Sprinkle the finished dish with the finely chopped peppermint (savory) and parsley.

<u>**Serve with:**</u> *Boston Salad*

33.2. BOSTON SALAD

Ingredients for 4 servings:

- 1 Butterhead Salad
- 4 oz. (113 g.) Baby Spinach

- 3 green onions
- 12 oz. (340 g.) Russet Potatoes
- 8 olives

Spices: 2 tablespoons oil, 2 tablespoons finely chopped parsley, 2 tablespoons lemon juice, salt to taste.

Way of preparation:

Boil the potatoes, cut them into small cubes. Clean, wash and finely chop the onion and spinach. Shred washed salad. Add them to the potatoes. Add salt to your taste. Sprinkle with oil, lemon juice and parsley. Decorate the salad with olives.

34.1. FISH SOUP WITH CHILI PEPPER

Ingredients for 4 servings:

- 11 oz. (312 g.) White Fish Fillets
- 1 medium carrot
- ½ cup celery
- 3 green onions
- 2 tablespoons chopped tomatoes
- 2 tablespoon sunflower oil
- 2 chili peppers

Spices: 2 sprigs thyme or dried thyme, lemon juice, ground black pepper and salt to taste.

Way of preparation:

Cut the cleaned and washed fish pieces. Allow them to stand 10 minutes sprinkled with salt, pepper, thyme and tomatoes.

Finely chop the onion, carrot, celery and chili peppers. Drop them in boiling salted water   (4 cups). When they become soft - add the fish and oil. Simmer for additional 10 minutes.

When serving - season the soup with ground black pepper and lemon juice.

Serve with: *Trout Baked in Parchment Paper*

34.2. TROUT BAKED IN PARCHMENT PAPER

Ingredients for 4 servings:
- 4 Small Trout
- 4 teaspoons olive oil
- 4 cloves of garlic
- 4 slices of lemon
- parchment paper

Spices: 2 tablespoons finely chopped parsley, salt to taste.

Way of preparation:
Salt the fishes inside and out. In each fish place the mixture of finely chopped parsley and garlic. Grease the fishes with olive oil. Wrap each fish separately in greased with olive oil parchment paper. Arrange packages in a greased baking dish and bake in a moderately hot oven 390 F / 200 C, about 30 minutes. Serve the fish hot, on the paper. Garnish with lemon slices.

35.1. CHICKEN BREAST WITH RED WINE

Ingredients for 4 servings:
- 1 lb. 8 oz. (680 g.) Chicken Breast
- 2 sweet onions
- 2 cloves garlic
- 1 teaspoon of tomato paste
- 2 tablespoons sunflower oil
- ½ cup dry red wine

Spices: 2 tablespoons chopped parsley, ½ tablespoon dried thyme, 1 chilli pepper, ground black pepper and salt to taste.

Way of preparation:
Cut the chicken breast into portions. Add salt and season it with pepper. Smother the meat with hot oil. Add cut into small cubes onion and garlic. Smother them gently and add half of the wine with dissolved in it tomato paste and ½ cup water. Pour mixture in a tray, sprinkle with parsley and thyme. Cover with the lid and roast 20 minutes in a moderately heated oven 392 F / 200 C. Cut the chilli pepper and add it to the dish, add the remaining wine.

Again cover with the lid and bake another 10 minutes. Serve hot, garnish with loose leaf lettuce.

Combines with:

Vegetable salads and vegetable soups - without potatoes; to them may be added meat, chicken, ham, mushrooms, olives (prepared according to the recipes of this book).

36.1. FRIED POACHED EGGS WITH A SAUCE OF WALNUTS

Ingredients for 1 serving:
- 3 large eggs
- ½ teaspoon sunflower oil

For the sauce: 1 clove garlic, ½ teaspoon vinegar, 1 ½ teaspoon ground walnuts.

Spices: ground black pepper and salt to taste.

Way of preparation:

Heat the pan. Put the oil. Top crush the eggs, being careful not to spill. Sprinkle with pepper and salt. Fry them on medium heat until they became densely.

Serve eggs flights with sauce made from: crushed garlic, salt, vinegar and chopped walnuts.

Serve with: *Baby Spinach Salad with Rucola*

36.2. BABY SPINACH SALAD WITH RUCOLA

Ingredients for 4 servings:
- 11 oz. (312 g.) raw Baby Spinach
- 1 cup Rucola
- 3 green onion
- 1 fresh green garlic
- 1 boiled egg
- 10 black olives

Spices: 5 sprigs of chopped parsley, 2 tablespoons olive oil, 1 tablespoon vinegar, ground black pepper and salt to taste.

Way of preparation:

Wash the spinach and Rucola thoroughly with cold water. Add finely chopped onion, garlic and parsley. Season the salad with salt, pepper, vinegar and olive oil. Peel the egg and cut it into slices. Cover the salad with them. Sprinkle with olive oil. Decorate the salad with olives.

37.1. LAMB CUTLETS WITH CARROTS

Ingredients for 4 servings:
- 8 Lamb Chops
- 24 baby carrots
- 1 yellow onion
- ½ cup white wine
- 2 cloves of garlic
- 2 tablespoons of sunflower oil

Spices: 2 tablespoons finely chopped parsley, ground black pepper and salt to taste.

Way of preparation:
Cut the onion on slices. Put them in pan and add 1 tablespoon oil and smother the carrots with the onion. Add pepper and salt. Pour ½ cup of hot water and wine. Cover up with the lid and leave another 10 minutes to stew.

Rub the cutlets with the crushed garlic. Sprinkle with salt and pepper. Smother them lightly in a pan with the remaining oil. Add them to the vegetable mixture. Allow the dish to boil on low heat for 30 minutes.

<u>*Serve with*</u>: *Salad of Fresh Purslane*

37.2. SALAD OF FRESH PURSLANE

Ingredients for 4 servings:
- 1 Bunch Purslane
- 3 green onions
- 2 green garlic
- 3 tablespoons lemon juice

- 2 tablespoons olive oil
- 10 black olives

Spices: 2 tablespoons finely chopped dill, 4 lemon slices, salt to taste.

Way of preparation:

Clean and wash the Purslane. Cut the purslane, onion and garlic into finely. Add olives, dill, olive oil, lemon juice and salt to taste. Serve the salad decorated with lemon slices. Serve immediately.

38.1. CHICKEN BREAST WITH GREEN ONION

Ingredients for 4 servings:

- 4 Chicken Breast
- 6 oz. (170 g.) green onions
- ½ cup white wine
- 2 tablespoons sunflower oil
- 1 teaspoon of tomato paste

Spices: 1 teaspoon paprika, 2 tablespoons chopped parsley, 7 peppercorns, 2 bay leaf leaves, salt to taste.

Way of preparation:

Cut the chicken breasts into portions. Smother them in oil, add chopped onions. After 10 minutes, sprinkle with paprika, and stir. Add the tomato puree, the wine, the peppercorns, ½ cup of hot water and salt to taste. Let the meat simmer about 30 minutes.

Finally, sprinkle with parsley. Serve warm with fresh vegetable salad.

<u>Combines with:</u>

Vegetable salads and vegetable soups - without potatoes; to them may be added meat, chicken, ham, mushrooms, olives (prepared according to the recipes of this book).

39.1. ROASTED CATFISH FILLET

Ingredients for 4 servings:

- 26 oz. (737 g.) Fresh Catfish Fillet

- 1 yellow onion
- 2 ribs celery
- 2 tablespoon sunflower oil
- ½ cup diced tomatoes
- 8 green olives

Spices: 2 cloves, 2 tablespoons finely chopped parsley, ground black pepper and salt to taste.

Way of preparation:

Arrange the fish in a greased baking dish with oil. Cut the onion into slices and smother in oil. After 4 minutes, add the diced celery and cloves. Smother until a thick paste. Add the finely chopped parsley, tomatoes, olives, black pepper and salt. Mix and spread the mixture over the fish. Cover the pan with foil. Bake the fish in moderate oven 392 F / 200 C, about 30 minutes.

Combines with:

Vegetable salads and vegetable soups - without potatoes; to them may be added fish, seafood, fish caviar, mushrooms, olives (prepared according to the recipes of this book).

40.1. CHICKEN WINGS IN AN OVEN

Ingredients for 4 servings:

- 20 Chicken Wings

Spices: 2 tablespoons oil, 3 tablespoons lemon juice, 2 tablespoons tomato sauce, 2 teaspoons paprika, ground black pepper and salt to taste.

Way of preparation:

Place in a deep bowl all the spices. Mix them well. Add to them the chicken wings. Allow to stand for 2 hours in the refrigerator.

Preheat a baking tray and place the wings. Bake 40 minutes until the wings turn golden brown.

Serve the wings hot, with butter head salad.

Combines with:

Vegetable salads and vegetable soups - without potatoes; to them may be added chicken, meat, ham, mustard, mushrooms, olives (

prepared according to the recipes of this book).

41.1. SOUP OF SPINACH WITH CHICKPEAS

Ingredients for 4 servings:
- 9 oz. (225 g.) fresh spinach
- 1 cup boiled chickpeas
- 3 green onions
- 2 tablespoons oil

Spices: 1 teaspoon paprika, 2 tablespoons chopped parsley and dill, 2 tablespoons lemon juice, ground black pepper and salt to taste.

Way of preparation:
Smother spinach in oil with chopped onions. Sprinkle with paprika and salt. Add boiled chickpeas and 4 cups of hot water. Cook the soup for 10 minutes.

Serve sprinkled with parsley, dill and black pepper. Optionally each serve could be seasoned with lemon juice.

 Serve with: *Pinto Beans Roasted in the Oven*

41.2. PINTO BEANS ROASTED IN THE OVEN

Ingredients for 4 servings:
- 2 cups boiled beans
- 2 tablespoons sunflower oil
- 1 yellow onion
- 1 medium carrot
- 3 mini sweet peppers

Spices: 2 teaspoons paprika, ½ teaspoon oregano, 4 slices of lemon, salt to taste.

Way of preparation:
Cut the onion finely. Smother it in oil. Add the sliced on rings carrots, mini sweet peppers and the spices. After 2 minutes, add the beans, oregano and 1 cup hot water. Stir well. Pour the mixture into a baking dish. Bake the dish at 392 F / 200 C, until

crusted. Once cool, arrange the lemon slices on top.

42.1. LAMB WITH CURRY SAUCE

Ingredients for 4 servings:
- 1 lb. 8 oz. (680 g.) Lamb Meat
- 2 sweet onions
- 2 cloves of garlic
- 1 teaspoon shredded ginger
- 1 tablespoon ground walnuts
- 3 tablespoons of sunflower oil
- 3 tablespoons lemon juice

Spices: 1 teaspoon curry, 1 teaspoon paprika, ¼ teaspoon nutmeg, ground black pepper and salt to taste.

Way of preparation:

Mix the curry, nutmeg, black pepper, paprika, garlic, salt, lemon juice and 2 tablespoons of sunflower oil. Mix the mixture well. Rub the lamb with it. Leave it in the fridge for 2 hours

Cut the onion finely. Smother it with ginger in oil. Add ground walnuts, the rest of the spice mix and 1 cup hot water. Put this sauce in the baking pan. Place the meat on it. Cover it with foil. Bake the meat in a moderately hot oven 356 F / 180 C, until soft. Serve warm with fresh vegetable salad.

Combines with:

Vegetable salads and vegetable soups - without potatoes; to them may be added meat, chicken, ham, mushrooms, olives (prepared according to the recipes of this book).

43.1. FISH FILLET WITH FENNEL

Ingredients for 4 servings:
- 1 lb. 8 oz. (680 g.) fish fillet
- 1 cup fennel, cut into thin strips
- 9 oz. (255 g.) whole small mushrooms
- 2 cloves of garlic, finely chopped

- 3 tablespoons lemon juice
- 3 tablespoons of sunflower oil

Spices: 10 sprigs of parsley, 10 sprigs of dill, ground black pepper and salt to taste.

Way of preparation:

Clean and wash the fish fillet. Sprinkle them with lemon juice. Leave the fish fillet to stand 10-15 minutes. Salt them. Smother the mushrooms, fennel and garlic with oil. Salt them, sprinkle them with pepper. Pour half of the mushroom mixture in a baking dish. Arrange the fish fillet on top. Put them on other mushrooms. Fill up with ½ cup of hot water. Roast the dish in a moderately high heat until it remains on fat, about 30 minutes, 392 F / 200 C. Before serving, put on each fillet sprinkle it with finely chopped parsley and dill.

Combines with:

Vegetable salads and vegetable soups - without potatoes; to them may be added fish, seafood, fish caviar, mushrooms, olives (prepared according to the recipes of this book).

44.1.BEEF SOUP

Ingredients for 4 servings:
- 14 oz. (400 g.) Boneless Beef
- 1 large carrot
- 2 parsley roots
- 1 yellow onion
- 1 teaspoon grated ginger
- 1 tablespoon oil
- 1 teaspoon tomato paste

Spices: 2 tablespoons chopped parsley, 4 tablespoons lemon juice, ground black pepper and salt to taste.

Way of preparation:

Wash the veal and cut it into small pieces. Pour over it 5-6 cups of cold water. When it starts to boil, reduce the heat and keep removing the foam. When the meat is almost cooked, add the onion, ginger, parsley root and chopped carrots, tomato paste and salt. Allow the soup to simmer for 25 minutes. Serve the soup hot. Sprinkled with chopped parsley and black pepper. Season it as desired with lemon juice.

Combines with:

Vegetable salads and vegetable dishes - without potatoes; to them may be added meat, chicken, ham, mushrooms, olives (prepared according to the recipes of this book).

45.1. CHICKEN BREAST WITH CUMIN SAUCE

Ingredients for 4 servings:
- 4 Boneless Skinless Chicken Breast
- 2 large carrots
- 2 garlic cloves
- 1 teaspoon of grated ginger
- 1 teaspoon cumin
- 2 tablespoons olive oil

Spices: ground black pepper and salt to taste.

Way of preparation:

Rub Chicken Breast with ground black pepper and salt. Scrape the carrots and garlic.

Smother in a pan the ginger, the carrots and garlic for 5 minutes with 1 tablespoon olive oil. Remove them from the pan. Fill up the remaining olive oil. Put the chicken breast. Turn them round until they become golden brown. Remove the chicken from the pan and arrange on a large plate.

Return the stewed vegetables into the pan. Add cumin, ½ cup of hot water. Simmer the sauce until thickened about 10 minutes. Pour over chicken breast with warm sauce.

Combines with:

Vegetable salads and vegetable soups - without potatoes; to them may be added meat, chicken, ham, mushrooms, olives (prepared according to the recipes of this book).

46.1. OMELETTE WITH MOTLEY STUFFING

Ingredients for 1 serving:
- 3 large eggs
- 3 black olives pitted
- 1 small pickled cucumber
- ¼ cup fresh mushrooms
- 2 teaspoons sunflower oil
- 2 leaves of lettuce

Spices: 2 sprigs of dill, ground black pepper and salt to taste.

Way of preparation:
Clean, wash and finely chop the mushrooms. Smother them with 1 teaspoon oil. When soft, add the chopped olives (pitted) and pickle. Season it with salt, pepper and fine chopped dill.
Separately fry plain omelet, add the filling, fold in half. Serve the omelet warm on a leaves of lettuce.

Combines with:
Vegetable salads, vegetable soups and vegetable dishes - without potatoes; to them may be added eggs, mushrooms, olives (prepared according to the recipes of this book).

47.1. SPINACH WITH FRESH POTATOES

Ingredients for 4 servings:
- 1 lb. (454 g.) fresh spinach
- ½ cup finely chopped onion
- 28 oz. (800 g.) fresh potatoes, cut into thin slices
- 3 tablespoons oil

Spices: ½ teaspoon oregano, ground black pepper and salt to taste.

Way of preparation:
Clean, wash and smother the spinach and onion over a low heat with 1 tablespoon oil. Sprinkle with black pepper and oregano In a baking dish place a row of spinach - a row of peeled and cut into thin slices potatoes and 1 cup salted water. Top sprinkle the dish with 2 tablespoons oil. Bake for about 40 minutes in a pre-heated

oven to 392 F / 200 C.

Combines with:

Vegetable salads and vegetable soups - to them may be added potatoes, mushrooms, olives (prepared according to the recipes of this book).

48.1. AROMATIC FISH SOUP

Ingredients for 4 servings:
- 11 oz. (312 g.) fish fillet
- 4 oz. (113 g.) fresh or pickled mushrooms
- 1 medium carrot, peeled and sliced
- ½ cup green onions, finely chopped
- ½ cup fennel, finely chopped
- 2 tablespoons sunflower oil

Spices: 1 tablespoon finely chopped dill, 2 tablespoons finely chopped parsley, 2 tablespoons lemon juice, ground black pepper and salt to taste.

Way of preparation:

Sauté the carrots and fennel in hot oil. Add 5 cups hot salted water. Cook them 10 minutes.

Add the chopped fish fillets, cleaned and sliced mushrooms and green onion. Keep cooking for an additional 5 minutes. Season the soup with ground black pepper, lemon juice and sprinkle with chopped dill and parsley.

Serve with: *Fish Meatballs*

48.2. FISH MEATBALLS

Ingredients for 4 servings:
- 26 oz. (737 g.) fish fillet
- ½ cup green onions, finely chopped
- 4 tablespoons of sunflower oil
- 1 tablespoon sesame seeds

Spices: 2 tablespoons finely chopped parsley, 1 teaspoons dried lavage, 4 slice of lemon, 4 lettuce leaves, ground black pepper and salt to taste.

Way of preparation:

Mince the fish fillets. Add the onion, parsley and lovage. Season the mixture with pepper and salt. Knead the fish mixture, adding oil on drops. Shape meatballs, roll them in sesame seeds. Put them in an oiled baking dish. Pour them with remaining oil. Bake meatballs until browned. Serve them on the leaves of lettuce with a slice of lemon.

49.1. LAMB RIBS WITH MUSTARD

Ingredients for 4 servings:
- 2 pieces by 8 lamb ribs

Spices: 1 tablespoon tomato sauce, 1 tablespoon mustard, 2 tablespoon grapeseed oil, paprika, ground black pepper and salt to taste.

Way of preparation:

Prepare a mixture of all spices. Smear the lamb ribs well with this mixture. Arrange the ribs in a tray with the fat part up. Pour ½ cup of hot water in the pan. Cover it with a foil and bake in a moderately hot oven 374 F / 190 C, 60 minutes at. Cut the ribs into portions. Serve them warm with fresh vegetable salad.

Combines with:

Vegetable salads and vegetable soups - without potatoes; to them may be added meat, chicken, ham, mushrooms, olives (prepared according to the recipes of this book).

50.1. SPINACH SOUP WITH RICE

Ingredients for 4 servings:
- 11 oz. (312 g.) fresh spinach
- ½ cup rice
- 1 tablespoon tomato paste
- 3 green onion

- 4 cups hot water
- 2 tablespoons sunflower oil

Spices: 2 tablespoons finely chopped parsley, 1 tablespoons finely chopped spearmint leaves, ground black pepper and salt to taste.

Way of preparation:

Clean, wash and finely chop the spinach and onion. Pour over the hot water, add the oil and salt. After 5 minutes, add the cleaned and washed rice and tomato paste. Simmer about 20 minutes. Season the finished soup with black pepper, parsley and spearmint.

Serve with: *Salad with Avocado and Buckwheat*

50.2. SALAD WITH AVOCADO AND BUCKWHEAT

Ingredients for 4 servings:

- 1 Butterhead Lettuce
- 4 tablespoons uncooked buckwheat
- 1 salad tomato
- 2 large avocado
- 2 tablespoons finely chopped parsley

For the dressing: 2 tablespoons lemon juice, 2 tablespoons olive oil, 4 sprigs fresh cilantro, ground black pepper and salt to taste. Prepare the dressing, stirring all the ingredients to form a homogeneous mixture.

Way of preparation:

Put in a saucepan 1 cup of cold water. Add salt and buckwheat. Allow to simmer for 5 minutes. Then remove and rinse thoroughly with cold water. Drain it into a colander.

Wash the butterhead lettuce and then tear to pieces. Cut the tomatoes and the avocado into thin slices. Arrange the salad leaves in a large bowl. Put on the buckwheat on the butterhead lettuce. Arrange slices on her the slices of avocado and tomatoes. Sprinkle with parsley. Pour over the salad with dressing.

51.1.CHICKEN ROASTED IN PARCHMENT PAPER

Ingredients for 4 servings:
- 4 Boneless Chicken Breast
- 4 green onions
- 4 cloves of garlic
- 4 teaspoons oil

Spices: 1 teaspoon curcuma (Turmeric powder), ½ teaspoon ground coriander, ½ teaspoon ground nutmeg, ground black pepper and salt to taste.

Way of preparation:

Cut the chicken breasts into small pieces. Mix them well with the finely chopped onion and all spices. Prepare 4 sheets of paper. In every sheet paper pur ¼ of the mixture, 1 clove garlic and 1 teaspoon oil . Wrap the paper so as to form the packet. Press them gently by hand to make them flat. Arrange them in a baking dish. Pour some hot water. Roast in a very hot oven first 10 minutes, 426 F / 220 C. Then bake for another 25 minutes in a moderate oven 372 F / 190 C. You can roast on grill, also.

Serve each packet in a separate dish, being careful in opening not to expire a sauce.

<u>**Combines with:**</u>

Vegetable salads and vegetable soups - without potatoes; to them may be added meat, chicken, ham, mushrooms, olives (prepared according to the recipes of this book).

52.1. CODFISH FILLET IN ITALIAN WAY

Ingredients for 4 servings:
- 1 lb. 12 oz. (800 g.) Codfish Fillet
- 12 basil leaves
- 2 red tomatoes
- 2 cloves of garlic
- 2 tablespoons olive oil
- 1 tablespoon chili sauce
- 3 oz. (85g.) small tin anchovies

Spices: ground black pepper and salt to taste.

Way of preparation:

Grease Codfish Fillet on both sides with chili sauce. Arrange them in a greased tray with olive oil. Arrange tomatoes on top, cut into rings. Sprinkle with chopped basil and crushed garlic. Put the fillets of anchovies on the top. Sprinkle with olive oil. Place the tray in a moderately heated oven 392 F / 200 C. Bake the dish for 20 minutes. Serve warm with fresh vegetable salad.

Combines with:

Vegetable salads and vegetable soups - without potatoes; to them may be added fish, seafood, fish caviar, mushrooms, olives (prepared according to the recipes of this book).

53.1. STEW PEAS

Ingredients for 4 servings:
- 2 cup cooked green peas
- 1 medium carrot
- 4 green onions
- 3 cloves of garlic
- 1 tablespoon tomato sauce
- ½ tablespoon grated ginger
- 2 tablespoons sunflower oil

Spices: 2 teaspoons paprika, 6 sprigs of dill, salt to taste.

Way of preparation:

Smother the finely chopped carrots, onions, garlic and ginger in oil. Add the tomato sauce and 1-2 tablespoons of water. When the water is boiled away, add paprika, and stir. Pour the peas. Salt and cook until remains on fat. Finally, sprinkle with finely chopped dill.

Combines with:

Vegetable salads and vegetable soups - to them may be added pulses, mushrooms, olives (prepared according to the recipes of this book).

54.1. *SOUP OF BEEF WITH GREEN BEANS*

Ingredients for 4 servings:
- 14 oz. (400 g.) Boneless Beef Stew Meat
- ½ cup green beans, cut into thin strips
- ½ cup onion, finely chopped
- ½ cup sliced fresh mushrooms
- ½ cup carrots, cut into thin strips
- 2 tablespoons grapeseed oil
- ½ tablespoon tomato paste

Spices: 2 tablespoons finely chopped parsley, 4 tablespoons lemon juice, ground black pepper and salt to taste.

Way of preparation:

Smother with oil into another utensil the green beans, onion, mushrooms, carrots, tomato paste and salt.

Pour over the meat it 5 cups cold water. When it starts to boil, reduce the heat and keep removing the foam. When the meat is almost cooked, add the smothered mixture to it. Allow the soup to simmer for 20 minutes. Serve the soup hot, sprinkled with chopped parsley and black pepper. Season it as desired with lemon juice.

<u>Combines with:</u>

Vegetable salads and vegetable dishes - without potatoes; to them may be added meat, chicken, ham, mushrooms, olives (prepared according to the recipes of this book).

55.1. *SPINACH SOUFFLE*

Ingredients for 4 servings:
- 1 lb. 6 oz. (624 g.) fresh spinach
- 6 egg whites
- 1 clove crushed garlic
- 1 tablespoons butter

Spices: ¼ teaspoon grated nutmeg, ground black pepper and salt to taste.

Way of preparation:
Heat in a saucepan the butter. Add to it the garlic and the spinach. Cover and simmer until tender. Then sprinkle with salt, nutmeg and pepper. Remove the pan from the fire.

Beat the egg whites with salt on snow. Very carefully add them to the spinach. The resulting mixture is poured into trays for soufflé, which are previously spread with butter. The trays shall be placed in a large baking dish filled with water to the edge of the trays. Place in preheated oven at 356 F / 180 C. Roast the soufflé approximately 25 minutes. Serve warm.

Serve with: *Lettuce Salad with Egg*

55.2.. LETTUCE SALAD WITH EGG

Ingredients for 4 servings:
- 2 Romaine Lettuces
- 4 green onions
- 1 green garlic
- 1 hard-boiled egg
- 8 black olives

Spices: 6 sprigs of parsley, 3 tablespoons olive oil, salt and vinegar to taste.

Way of preparation:
Shred the cleaned and washed salads and put them in a large bowl. Add the chopped onions and garlic. Sprinkle with finely chopped parsley, olive oil and vinegar. Mix the salad. On her order egg cut into rings. Arrange the egg, sliced into rings on the top. Decorate the salad with olives.

56.1. MUSHROOM "ASORTI" WITH CHEESE

Ingredients for 4 servings:
- 1 lb. 8 oz. (680 g.) different kinds of fresh mushrooms
- ½ cup onions, finely chopped
- 2 cloves of crushed garlic

- 1 teaspoon butter
- ½ cup of white wine
- 1 cup sour cream
- ½ cup Grated Cheddar Cheese

Spices: 1 teaspoon thyme, 6 sprigs parsley, ground black pepper and salt to taste.

Way of preparation:

Cut the mushrooms on large pieces. Sprinkle them with salt and pepper. Smother them in butter with the onion. Allow the mixture to stew 7 minutes. At the end add the chopped garlic and wine. Once the water has evaporated, add the cream, thyme and parsley, stir. Transfer the mixture into a baking dish. Sprinkle with grated Cheddar Cheese. Bake 15 minutes in a moderately heated oven, 392 F / 200 C. Serve warm.

Serve with: Lettuce Salad with Sunflower Seeds

56.2. LETTUCE SALAD WITH SUNFLOWER SEEDS

Ingredients for 4 servings:

- 1 Romaine lettuce
- 1 cup Baby Spinach
- ½ cup red onion, finely chopped
- 2 tablespoons raw hulled sunflower seeds
- 1 oz. (28 g.) Parmesan Cheese, finely shredded

Spices: 2 tablespoons olive oil, 2 tablespoons lemon juice, 1 teaspoon mustard, salt and ground black pepper to taste.

Way of preparation:

Put sunflower seeds in a pan without oil and roast for a few minutes as to enhance flavor. Shaking the pan frequently. In a large bowl mix chopped salad, baby spinach and red onion.

Separately mix all spices. Put the dressing on the salad. Sprinkle with sunflower seeds and grated parmesan cheese.

57.1. GROUND WHITE TURKEY MEATBALLS

Ingredients for 4 servings:

- 1 lb. 10 oz. (737 g.) Ground White Turkey
- 3 tablespoons oil
- 3 green onion, finely chopped
- 2 mini sweet papers, finely chopped

Spices: 2 teaspoon Worcestershire Sauce, 2 tablespoons finely chopped parsley, 1 teaspoon Italian Seasoning, ground black pepper and salt to taste.

Way of preparation:

Put in a deep boil of ground white turkey. Add the onions, mini peppers, 1 tablespoon oil and spices to it. Knead the minced meat; gradually add 3 tablespoons of water.

Smear your hands with oil and shape into medium meatballs. Put them to bake in a preheated pan greased with oil. Sprinkle with oil and roast until browned: 30 minutes, 392 F / 200 C.

Serve with: *Salad of Chicory with Red Onion*

57.2. SALAD OF CHICORY WITH RED ONION

Ingredients for 4 servings:

- 1 lb. (454 g.) Fresh Chicory
- 4 Cherry Tomatoes
- 1 red onion, cut into thin strips
- 12 green olives

For the dressing: 1 clove garlic, 2 tablespoons olive oil, 1 teaspoon mustard, 2 tablespoons lemon juice, 5 finely chopped mint leaves, salt to taste.

Way of preparation:

First, prepare the dressing. Put all ingredients in a bowl and stir them vigorously. Leave it in the refrigerator while you prepare the salad.

Wash the chicory and cut it into thin strips. Put in a boil of chicory, onions, whole cherry tomatoes and chopped green olives. Pour over the salad with the dressing. Serve it cold.

58.1. ROASTED CHICKEN DRUMSTICKS WITH SPICY SAUCE

Ingredients for 4 servings:
  ✓   8 Chicken Drumsticks

For the marinade: 1/2 cup white wine 1 teaspoon of balsamic vinegar, 2 cloves garlic finely chopped, 1 tablespoon oil, 6 peppercorns

For the sauce: 1 teaspoon of butter, 2 sweet onions, ½ cup wine, 1 teaspoon balsamic vinegar, 1 teaspoon mustard, 3 pickled gherkins, 2 tablespoons chopped parsley, ground black pepper and salt to taste.

Way of preparation:

Preparation of marinade: Mix all products. Stir them well.

Place the chicken drumsticks in a deep bowl and pour with the prepared marinade. Allow to stand in refrigerator 1-2 hours. Drain the legs and roast them on the grill or in the oven.

Preparation of the sauce: Put in a pre-heated pan the butter and the chopped onions. Add ½ cup wine and 1 teaspoon balsamic vinegar. Sprinkle with ground black pepper. Let the mixture simmer for 10 minutes. Remove from the heat. Then add the mustard, finely sliced parsley and chopped cucumbers.

Before serving, pour the chicken drumsticks with sauce.

Combines with:

Vegetable salads and vegetable soups - without potatoes; to them may be added meat, chicken, ham, mushrooms, olives (prepared according to the recipes of this book).

59.1. LAMB WITH MINT

Ingredients for 4 servings:
  • 1 lb. 8 oz. (680 g.) Lamb Stew Meat
  • 1 yellow onion
  • 4.5 oz. (120 g.) petite diced tomatoes
  • 6 green pitted olives
  • 2 tablespoons sunflower oil

Spices: 4 mint leaves, ground black pepper and salt to taste.

Way of preparation:

Heat the oil, put the meat and onion, smother. Stir the dish a few times. After 10 minutes, add salt, pepper, tomatoes and 1 – 1 ½ cups of hot water. Cover the pan with the lid and leave the dish on low heat. When the meat is tender, add the mint. Serve warm.

<u>*Serve with:*</u> *Purslane Salad with Walnuts*

59.2. PURSLANE SALAD WITH WALNUTS

Ingredients for 4 servings:

- 2 bunch Purslane, cut into thin strips
- 3 green onions, finely chopped
- 2 green garlic, finely chopped
- 2 tablespoons ground walnuts

Dressing: 1 tablespoon vinegar, 2 tablespoons sunflower oil, salt to taste.

Way of preparation:

First, prepare the dressing. Put all ingredients in a bowl and stir them vigorously.

Put in a boil of purslane, onions and garlic, stir. Pour over the salad with the dressing. Sprinkle with the walnuts. Serve it cold.

60.1. WHITE FISH IN GELATIN

Ingredients for 4 servings:

- 21 oz. (600 g.) fillet of white fish
- 20 g. Unflavored Gelatin
- 1 sweet onion
- 1 large carrot
- 2 ribs celery
- 2 parsley roots
- 2 bay leaves

Spices: ground black pepper and salt to taste.

Decoration: sliced lemon, marinated cucumber cut into circles, leaves parsley.

Way of preparation:

In a saucepan with 4 cups of water put to boil the fish, onion, carrots, celery, parsley root, bay leaves and salt (20 minutes). Arrange the cooked fish in a large tray. Arrange sliced carrots on the fish .

Mix the gelatin with cold water and leave to swell. Strain the broth in which you boiled the fish and carefully add it to the swollen gelatin. When the mixture begins to cool and slightly thickened, pour the cold fish. Put fish dish in the refrigerator until the gelatin completely tighten.

Serve the fish cold, decorated with sliced lemon, marinated cucumber cut into circles, leaves parsley.

Combines with:

Vegetable salads and vegetable soups, dishes - without potatoes; to them may be added fish, seafood, fish caviar, mushrooms, olives (prepared according to the recipes of this book).

SUMMER - LUNCH

1.1. STUFFED ZUCCHINI WITH GROUND BEEF

Ingredients for 4 servings:
- 2 large thick zucchini
- 11 oz. (312 g.) ground beef
- 1 medium onion
- 1 medium carrot
- 1 large tomato
- 2 tablespoons vegetable oil

Spices: 2 tablespoons finely chopped parsley, 1 tablespoon finely chopped dill, 4 sprigs dill – for decoration, ground black pepper and salt to taste.

Way of preparation:

Preheat the oven to 392 F / 200 C.

Wash the zucchini, cut them in half across. Carve them and finely chop ¼ of their inner part. Finely chop the onion, carrot and tomato. Put the oil in a deep pan. When it warms, add the onion and carrots to stew for 4-5 minutes. Add the ground beef. Stir until its color changes and shatters. Add the inside part of the zucchini, tomatoes, black pepper, a pinch of salt and ½ cup hot water. Leave the mixture to cook until the liquid evaporates. Then add the chopped dill and parsley. Remove the mixture from the stove. Stir it and fill the zucchini with it. Arrange them in a baking tray. Pour 1 cup of hot water and put the dish to bake for 30-40 minutes until the zucchini soften. Serve the zucchini warm, decorate them with a sprig of dill.

Serve with: *Tomato Salad with Basil*

1.2. TOMATO SALAD WITH BASIL

Ingredients for 4 servings:
- 4 large tomatoes
- 10-12 fresh basil leaves

For dressing: 1 tablespoon olive oil, 2 cloves crushed garlic, salt to taste.

Way of preparation:
Cut each tomato into 8 slices. Put them in a large bowl. Prepare the dressing in a bowl. Put the ingredients for the dressing and mix them vigorously. Sprinkle the salad with the dressing. On top add the fresh basil leaves. Serve the salad after its preparation.

2.1. CARROT CREAM SOUP

Ingredients for 4 servings:
- 1 lb. (454 g.) fresh carrots
- 7 oz. (200 g.) Russet Potatoes
- 1 small onion
- 3 - 4 ribs celery
- 1 teaspoon butter

Spices: 1 tablespoon finely chopped parsley, ground black pepper and salt to taste.

Way of preparation:
Boil the carrots, potatoes, onion and celery in 4 cups of water with a pinch of salt. After they soften enough, take them out with a slotted spoon and puree them. Put them back in the broth. Cook the soup for 2-3 more minutes. Then remove it from the stove and add the butter, parsley and black pepper. Serve the soup warm.
Serve with: *Meatballs of Zucchini and Potatoes*

2.2. MEATBALLS OF ZUCCHINI AND POTATOES

Ingredients for 4 servings:
- 2 lbs. (907 g.) Zucchini
- 14 oz. (400 g.) Russet Potatoes
- 2-3 green onions
- 4 tablespoons vegetable oil

Spices: 2 tablespoons finely chopped fresh dill, 2 tablespoons finely chopped parsley, ground black pepper and salt to taste.

Way of preparation:
Put the potatoes to boil with a pinch of salt for 20-25 minutes. Let them cool. Peel them and grate them coarsely. Cut the onion very finely.
Peel the zucchini, grate them coarsely. Sprinkle with salt. Leave them to stay for 30 minutes. Then drain them well. Put in a deep bowl the drained zucchini, potatoes, onions, spices and 2 tablespoons of oil. Knead the mixture, if necessary add a little more salt. Form the meatballs, arrange them in a baking tray greased with oil. Sprinkle the burgers with 2 tablespoons of oil. Preheat the oven to 392 F / 200 C. Place the tray in the oven. Bake the burgers for about 30-40 minutes.

3.1. STEW OF FRESH SEA FISH FILLETS

Ingredients for 4 servings:
- 2-3 Fresh Fillets Sea Breams (or other fresh fish)
- 2 Yellow Onions
- 2 Friggitelo Sweet red Peppers
- 3 Roma tomatoes
- 1-2 tablespoons olive oil
- 4 slices of lemon

Spices: 2 tablespoons finely chopped basil, 2 tablespoons finely chopped parsley, ground black pepper and salt to taste.
Way of preparation:
Select large fillets of fresh sea fish – sea bream (mackerel, bluefish, bonito or other fresh fish of your choice). Cut the fillets into pieces of 2 inch (5 cm.).
Clean the peppers from the seeds. Wash the vegetables and cut them into small cubes. Heat the olive oil in a wide pan and put the vegetables to stew for 10 minutes. Then add the fish fillets, salt and ground black pepper to taste. Put a lid and stew the dish on low heat for 15 minutes. Add the parsley, stir and remove the pan from the stove.
To each portion serve a slice of lemon, sprinkle with basil.

Serve with: *Cucumber Salad with Dill*

3.2. CUCUMBER SALAD WITH DILL

Ingredients for 4 servings:
- 1 lb. 8 oz. (680 g.) fresh cucumbers
- 1 small red onion
- 7-8 sprigs dill

For the dressing: 1-2 tablespoons olive oil, ½ tablespoon vinegar, salt to taste.

Way of preparation:
Peel and cut the cucumber into rings. Arrange them in serving plates, sprinkle them with finely chopped onion. Prepare the dressing from the olive oil, vinegar, and salt. Pour it over the salads and sprinkle with chopped dill. Serve immediately.

4.1. VEGETARIAN LASAGNA WITH CHEESE

Ingredients for 4 servings:
- 1 lb. (454 g.) eggplants
- 21 oz. (600 g.) green zucchini
- 3 oz. (85 g.) "Cheddar" cheese
- 3 oz. (85 g.) Smoked cheese, to your choice
- 3 oz. (85 g.) Blue cheese, to your choice
- 3 - 4 tablespoons oil

For the sauce: 1-2 tablespoons oil, 1 medium carrot, 1 lb. (454 g.) tomatoes, 1 onion, 1-2 cloves garlic, 1 handful fresh basil leaves (or 1 tablespoon dried basil), salt and ground black pepper to taste.

Way of preparation:
Cut the 3 types of cheese into thin slices.
Wash and cut into slices the zucchini and eggplant. Put them in two separate bowls and sprinkle them with salt. Leave them to stand for one hour. Then drain the zucchini and wash the eggplants with cold water. Drain them and dry them with kitchen

paper. Bake them in a "grill" non-stick pan for several minutes on each side. Put a few drops of oil on the bottom of the pan.

For the sauce: Chop finely the carrot, onion and garlic. Put them to stew in a deep pan with the oil. Peel and cut the tomatoes into small pieces. Add them in the pan. Leave the sauce to cook for 10 minutes. Add the spices and stir.

Divide the tomato sauce into three parts. Cover the bottom of a deep baking tray with 1/3 of the tomato sauce. Over it arrange the baked eggplant slices, then on them the baked zucchini. Over them put the other 1/3 of the tomato sauce. On it place ½ of the three types of cheese. Continue alternating eggplants and zucchini. Finish it with the last 1/3 tomato sauce and the remaining cheeses. Preheat the oven to 392 F / 200 C. Put the lasagna in the oven to bake for 20-30 minutes until the top crust. Serve the lasagna warm.

Serve with: *Purslane Salad with Yogurt*

4.2. PURSLANE SALAD WITH YOGURT

Ingredients for 4 servings:
- 2 bunch Fresh Purslane
- 1 cup Yogurt (whole milk)
- 1 tablespoon olive oil
- 1 cloves crushed garlic

Spices: 5-6 sprigs chopped dill, salt to taste, 8 olives and 4 sprigs of dill for decoration.

Way of preparation:
Put in a deep bowl the yogurt, olive oil and salt to taste. Stir the mixture well. Add the fresh purslane cut into thin strips, crushed garlic and dill, stir. Divide the salad into appropriate serving plates, garnish each serving with a sprig of dill and olive.

5.1. STEWED PORK CHOPS

Ingredients for 4 servings:

- 8 Center Cut Pork Chops
- 1 medium carrot
- 1 yellow onion
- 2-3 Friggitelo Sweet Peppers
- 2-3 cloves garlic
- ½ cup white wine
- 2 tablespoons vegetable oil

Spices: 1 teaspoon paprika, 1-2 bay leaves, 10 grains black pepper and salt to taste

Way of preparation:

Cut the carrots, onions and peppers into small thin slices. Using a meat mallet, pound the steaks lightly. Put them on a hot grill pan greased with oil. Turn them. After 5 minutes, remove them. In a separate pot stew the onion, garlic, carrots and peppers with oil. Sprinkle with paprika, pour the wine and 1 cup water. When the mixture starts to boil, put the steaks in it. Add the bay leaves, black pepper grains and salt. Cover the pot with a lid and leave the meat to stew on low heat for about 40 minutes. Serve the dish warm.

Combines with:

Vegetable salads and vegetable soups - without potatoes; to them may be added meat, chicken, ham, mushrooms, olives (prepared according to the recipes of this book).

6.1. SOUP OF BEEF RIB WITH HORSERADISH

Ingredients for 4 servings:
- 11 oz. (312 g.) Beef Rib for Soup
- 2 ribs celery
- 2 medium carrots
- 2 parsley roots
- 1 parsnips root

Spices: 1-2 bay leaves, 10-15 black pepper grains, 1 horseradish root, 5-6 tablespoons wine vinegar, 2 tablespoons finely chopped parsley, salt to taste.

Way of preparation:
Peel the vegetables and cut them into thin rings.
Wash the meat and put it in a deep pot. Pour it with 5-6 cups of cold water. Leave it to cook on low heat. When the water boils, remove the foam. After 1 hour, add the vegetables, salt, bay leaves, black pepper grains. Leave the soup to cook until the meat softens. Serve the soup warm. Sprinkle it with parsley.
Finely grate the horseradish. Put it in a small bowl, add the vinegar and stir the mixture vigorously. Serve this mixture to the soup. Everyone can add the preferred amount of it to the soup.
Serve with: *Okra Stew*

6.2. OKRA STEW

Ingredients for 4 servings:
- 21 oz. (595 g.) fresh okra
- 3 - 4 green onions
- 2 medium tomatoes
- 1-2 tablespoons vegetable oil

Spices: 1 teaspoon paprika, 2 sprigs fresh basil, 4 lemon slices, salt to taste.

Way of preparation:
Clean the okra. Cut its stalks. Pour the okra with hot water and a pinch of salt. Cook for 5-10 minutes. Drain it, and discard the water. In a separate pot heat the oil, put to stew consistently the onion, paprika, tomatoes and a pinch of salt. After 10 minutes, add the okra. Cook the dish on low heat for 10 minutes. Sprinkle it with basil before removing it from the stove. Serve the dish cold with lemon slices.

7.1. SOUP WITH SWEET PEAS AND RED BEANS

Ingredients for 4 servings:
- 1 cup sweet peas (boiled)
- 1 cup red beans (boiled)

- 1 small onion
- 1 medium carrot
- 2 ribs celery
- 2 cloves garlic
- ginger root - sized about 1-2 cm.
- 1-2 tablespoons vegetable oil

Spices: 2 sprigs fresh oregano, 1 tablespoon finely chopped parsley, ground black pepper and salt to taste.

Way of preparation:

Peel the ginger and grate it finely. Peel, wash and chop all the vegetables into small pieces. Put the oil in a deep pot. Add the onion, garlic and ginger. Stew them for 2 minutes. Pour them with 4-5 cups of hot water. Then add salt, carrots and celery. Cover the pot and let the soup to boil for 20 minutes. Add the peas and beans. Leave the soup to cook for another 5-6 minutes. Remove the pot from the stove. Sprinkle it with fresh oregano, parsley and black pepper. Serve the soup warm.

Serve with: *Salad with Radishes and Avocado*

7.2. SALAD WITH RADISHES AND AVOCADO

Ingredients for 4 servings:

- 1 Green Leaf Lettuce
- 5-6 radishes
- 1 large avocado
- 2-3 green onion
- 1 medium cucumber

Spices: 2 tablespoons olive oil, 2 tablespoons lemon juice, 2 tablespoons finely chopped parsley, salt to taste.

Way of preparation:

Cut the onion finely. Cover the bottom of a large plate with lettuce leaves. On it place layers of cut into rings cucumbers, avocado, internal lettuce leaves and on top – radishes, green onion and spices. Serve the salad immediately after its preparation.

8.1. COLD ITALIAN SOUP „GAZPACHO"

Ingredients for 4 servings:
- 1 lb. (454 g.) ripe tomatoes
- 2 - 3 Cubanelle Green Peppers
- 1 medium cucumber
- 1 small onion
- 2 cloves pressed garlic

Spices: 1 tablespoon olive oil, ½ tablespoon vinegar, 1-2 sprigs finely chopped fresh coriander, salt and ground black pepper to taste, 1 finely chopped chili pepper (optional)

Way of preparation:
Put in a deep bowl 1.75 pints (1 liter) of hot water. Dip the tomatoes for a few seconds. Remove them and cool them immediately. Peel them and put them in a blender. Clean the peppers from the seeds and stems. Wash them and put them in a blender. Add to them the onions and garlic. Turn on the blender for 10-15 seconds. Pour the vegetables in a deep bowl. Cut the cucumbers very finely. Add them to the bowl together with all the spices and 1-2 cups of cold water. Put a few ice cubes and serve. The soup is suitable for hot summer days.

Serve with: Spicy Boneless Chicken Breasts

8.2. SPICY BONELESS CHICKEN BREASTS

Ingredients for 4 servings:
- 4 Boneless chicken breasts
- 2 Sweet Red Peppers
- 1 large onion
- 3 cloves garlic
- 1-2 tablespoons tomato sauce
- 2 tablespoons vegetable oil

Spices: 1 tablespoon paprika, 1 teaspoon cumin, ground black pepper and salt to taste.

Way of preparation:
Cut very finely (you can use a blender) the peppers, onion and

garlic. Stew the onion lightly with the oil until it becomes translucent. Roll the chicken breasts in a mixture of garlic, paprika and tomato sauce. Put them into the onions and stew on low heat for 10-15 minutes. Then add to them the peppers, black pepper and salt. Leave the dish to simmer on low heat for 30-40 minutes. Pour a little of hot water, but the best is the chicken to stew in its own juice. Serve the dish warm.

9.1. AROMATIC PORK MEATBALLS

Ingredients for 4 servings:
- 26 oz. (737 g.) Ground Pork Meat
- 1 tablespoon vegetable oil

Spices: 1 tablespoon finely chopped parsley, 1 teaspoon thyme, 1 teaspoon mustard, ground black pepper and salt to taste.

Way of preparation:
In a deep bowl put the ground pork meat, spices and 2 tablespoons of cold water. Knead the mixture carefully. Cover it with foil. Put it into the refrigerator for several hours. Preheat the grill. Then grease your hands with oil and form meatballs. Place them on the grill. Turn them frequently until they turn crispy crust on both sides. Serve them warm.

Garnish them with fresh vegetables or vegetable sauces.

Serve with: Salad "Summer Mix"

9.2. SALAD "SUMMER MIX"

Ingredients for 4 servings:
- 3 medium tomatoes
- 1 green and 1 red sweet pepper
- 1 medium cucumber
- 1 red onion
- 1-2 chilies pepper (optional)

Spices: 3 tablespoons olive oil, 2 tablespoons finely chopped parsley, 5-6 fresh basil leaves, salt to taste.

Way of preparation:

Wash all the vegetables with cold water. Cut the tomatoes into 6-7 pieces. Cut the stems of the green and red peppers, and chilies. Cut them into 4 pieces lengthwise, remove the seeds, cut them into thin short strips. Peel the cucumber and cut it into rings. Peel the onion and chop finely. Put all the vegetables in a deep bowl. Add spices and mix. Serve the salad after its preparation.

10.1. SUMMER SOUP WITH SPINACH

Ingredients for 4 servings:
- 11 oz. (312 g.) fresh spinach
- 1 small onion
- 1 medium tomato
- 1 medium carrot
- 5-6 celery leaves
- ½ cup white short-grain rice
- 2 tablespoons vegetable oil

Spices: 2 tablespoons finely chopped fresh garden mint, 2-3 sprigs finely chopped dill, 5-6 sprigs finely chopped parsley, ground black pepper and salt to taste.

Way of preparation:

Peel and chop very finely the onion, carrots and celery. Put the oil in a pot to heat. Add the chopped vegetables, some water and salt. Stew the mixture on low heat. Then add the tomato – cut in small pieces. Leave the soup to cook for another 2-3 minutes. Pour the mixture with 5 cups of hot water and add the rice. Stir the soup and leave it to cook for another 15 minutes on low heat. Add the finely chopped fresh spinach. Continue cooking for another 5-7 minutes. Remove the pot from the stove and add the spices. Serve the soup warm.

Serve with: *Zucchini with Brown Rice*

10.2. *ZUCCHINI WITH BROWN RICE*

Ingredients for 4 servings:
- 21 oz. (600 g.) zucchini
- 1 cup brown rice
- 1 medium carrot
- 1 small onion
- 3 tablespoons vegetable oil

Spices: 1 tablespoon finely chopped dill, 1 tablespoon finely chopped parsley, ground black pepper and salt to taste

Way of preparation:
Put the rice in a deep pot and pour it with 3 cups of water. Add a pinch of salt and black pepper. Leave it to cook on low heat for 30-35 minutes.

Wash the zucchini and cut them into cubes of 0.8 inches (2 cm.). Peel the carrot and onion and cut them into small cubes. Put the oil in a deep pan. Heat it on low heat. Put the carrots and onion with a pinch of salt to stew for 10 minutes. Then add the zucchini. After 10 minutes, add the rice. Cover the pan with a lid and leave the dish to cook on low heat for 4-5 minutes. Add the dill and stir the dish. Remove it from the stove and serve it warm, sprinkle it with parsley.

11.1. *COD FISH WITH SAUCE OF ROASTED PEPPERS*

Ingredients for 4 servings:
- 1 lb. 12 oz. (800 g.) Cod fish Fillets with Skin
- 3 Red Cubanelle Peppers
- 1 tablespoon tomato sauce
- 2 sweet onions
- 1-2 cloves garlic
- 2 tablespoons olive oil

Spices: 1 bay leaf, ground black pepper and salt to taste.

Way of preparation:

Bake the peppers on grill, in oven or on stove. Put them to stew for 30 minutes in a bag. Then peel them, clean the seeds and cut them into thin strips of 0.8 inch (2 cm.).

Finely chop the onion and garlic. Cut the fish fillets into pieces. Sprinkle with salt and ground black pepper to taste. In a pan heat the olive oil on medium heat. Put the fillets skin side down. Do not turn the fillets. Remove them after 7-8 minutes. In the same oil add the onion and garlic to stew. After 2-3 minutes, add the tomato sauce, salt to taste and bay leaf. After 10 minutes, put in the pan with the sauce the roasted peppers and the stewed fish. Cook the dish for 5-6 minutes. Then serve it warm.

Combines with:

Vegetable salads and vegetable soups - without potatoes; to them may be added fish, seafood, fish caviar, mushrooms, olives (prepared according to the recipes of this book).

12.1. ZUCCHINI SOUP WITH QUINOA

Ingredients for 4 servings:
- 2 medium green zucchini
- 6 oz. (170 g.) fresh field mushrooms
- 2 fresh garlic
- 2 green onion
- 3 - 4 tablespoons quinoa
- 2 tablespoons vegetable oil

Spices: 2 tablespoons finely chopped dill, ground black pepper and salt to taste, the juice of 1 lemon (optional).

Way of preparation:
Peel and finely chop the zucchini, onion, garlic and mushrooms. Heat the oil and put them to stew for 10 minutes. Stir them occasionally. Add salt and black pepper. Stir the mixture and after 5 minutes add 4 cups of warm water and the quinoa. Leave the soup to cook on low heat for 10-15 minutes. Remove the pot from the stove. Sprinkle the soup with dill and serve it warm (optional serve lemon juice to the soup).

Serve with: *Stuffed Tomatoes with Rice*

12.2. STUFFED TOMATOES WITH RICE

Ingredients for 4 servings:
- 2 lbs. 10 oz. (1.190 g.) - 4 large tomatoes
- 2 tablespoons vegetable oil

For the filling: 2/3 cup rice, 3 green onions finely chopped, 2-3 tablespoons vegetable oil

Spices: 2 tablespoons finely chopped parsley, ground black pepper and salt to taste, 4 sprigs parsley.

Way of preparation:
Cut caps on top of the tomatoes. Carve their inner part with a small spoon. Prepare the filling: Heat the oil (2 tablespoons) in a deep pan. Put the onion and stew it for a few minutes on low heat. Then add the rice, stir and after 1-2 minutes add 1 ½ cup of water. When the rice absorbs the water, add ¼ of the carved inner part of the tomatoes. Sprinkle with salt, black pepper and parsley. Stir and remove the filling from the stove.

Stuff the tomatoes with the filling, put their caps on. Arrange the tomatoes in a baking tray. Preheat the oven to 392 F / 200 C. Pour the stuffed tomatoes with 2 tablespoons of oil. Put the tray in the oven. Bake the dish for 20 minutes. Serve it warm. For each portion serve 1 tomato. Garnish each serving with a sprig of parsley.

13.1. TOMATO SOUP WITH OKRA

Ingredients for 4 servings:
- 1 lb. (454 g.) ripe tomatoes
- 5 oz. (142 g.) fresh okra
- 2 green garlic
- 2 tablespoons grapeseed oil
- 1 large egg

Spices: 2 sprigs fresh basil, 1 teaspoon paprika, ground black pepper and salt to taste.

Way of preparation:
Clean the okra and cut it into small pieces. Peel and grate finely the tomatoes and garlic. Heat the oil and put them to stew for 10 minutes. Add the paprika, salt and okra. Pour them with 4 cups of hot water. Cook the soup for 10-15 minutes. Remove the soup from the stove and settle it with beaten egg. Sprinkle the soup with basil and black pepper. Serve it warm.

__Serve with:__ *French Beans with Egg Sauce*

13.2. FRENCH BEANS WITH EGG SAUCE

Ingredients for 4 servings:
- 1 lb. 8 oz. (680 g.) Fresh Green Beans
- 1 medium onion
- zest of ½ lemon

Spices: ground black pepper and salt to taste.

For the sauce: 2 egg yolks, 2-3 tablespoons vegetable oil, 2 tablespoons vinegar, ½ cup cold water.

Way of preparation:
Clean the green beans and wash them with cold water. Put it in a pot and pour over with 1 cup of water. Add salt, the finely chopped onion and lemon zest. Cook the green beans on low heat until soften. Prepare the sauce: Beat the egg yolks in a deep bowl with a mixer. Add the oil, water and vinegar. Stir the mixture over low heat until the sauce thickens. Pour it over the beans, stirring constantly. Cook the dish for only 2 more minutes. Remove it from the stove. Serve it warm, sprinkle it with black pepper.

14.1. CLASSIC CHICKEN SOUP

Ingredients for 4 servings:
- 1 Chicken Leg Quarter
- 1 small onion
- 1 medium carrot

- 2 ribs celery
- 1 teaspoon butter

Spices: 2 tablespoons finely chopped parsley, 6-7 black pepper grains, 1 bay leaf, ground black pepper and salt to taste.

Way of preparation:

Peel, wash and finely chop the onion, carrot and celery. Pour the chicken with 4 ½ cups of cold water. When the water starts boiling remove the foam. Boil the chicken until the meat begins to separate from the bones (about 30 minutes). Strain the broth. Remove the meat from the bones and discard the bones. Cut the meat into small pieces. Put in the broth the finely chopped vegetables, chicken, bay leaf, black pepper grains and salt to taste. Cook the soup for 20 minutes. Before remove it from the stove, add the butter and parsley. Serve the soup warm. Sprinkle it with ground black pepper.

Serve with: *Eggplant with Tomato Stuffing*

14.2. EGGPLANT WITH TOMATO STUFFING

Ingredients for 4 servings:
- 2 fresh large eggplants
- 1 teaspoon salt

For the filling: 3 tomatoes, 2 cloves garlic, 1-2 tablespoons vegetable oil, 1-2 tablespoons finely crushed walnuts, 2 tablespoons finely chopped parsley, 12 fresh basil leaves, ground black pepper and salt to taste.

Way of preparation:

Preheat the oven to 428 F / 220 C.

Wash the eggplants well and remove their stalks. Cut them into two halves along the length. Carefully carve each half. Put them in a deep bowl with the carved part. Sprinkle with salt and let them to stand for ½ hour. Then wash them thoroughly with cold water. Drain them and dry them. Chop finely the carved part of the eggplants.

Heat the oil in a deep pan. Finely chop the garlic and tomatoes.

Put the garlic in the pan and ½ part of the carved of the eggplants, salt and black pepper to taste. Stew them for 10-15 minutes on low heat. Then add the tomatoes. Cook until the filling thickens. Remove the pan from the stove, add the walnuts and parsley. Stir the filling and stuff the eggplants with it. Put them in a baking tray. Put to bake for about 30 minutes. Serve them warm. Garnish each serving with three basil leaves.

15.1. BBQ: SHORT PORK RIBS WITH ONION

Ingredients for 4 servings:
- 4 lbs. (1.820 g.) Short Pork Ribs
- 4 onions - cut in two

For the marinade: 2 cloves crushed garlic, 4 tomato sauce, ½ cup white wine, a pinch of ground nutmeg, 2 grains allspice, 1-2 cloves, a pinch of cinnamon, a pinch of ground black pepper, 1 tablespoon lemon zest.

Way of preparation:
First prepare the marinade. Put into suitable container the garlic, tomato sauce, wine, spices and lemon zest. Mix well. Put ribs in the marinade, pour them everywhere. Leave them to stand 2 hours in the refrigerator. Turn them occasionally. Then drain them well. Put them to bake on the grill for about 45 - 60 minutes. Turn them frequently as spreading with the marinade. Put the cut onions also on the grill at least 5-6 minutes before the ribs are ready. During roasting smear the onions with the marinade. Serve the ribs and onion warm.

Combines with:
Vegetable salads and vegetable soups - without potatoes; to them may be added meat, chicken, ham, mushrooms, olives (prepared according to the recipes of this book).

16.1. BEEF WITH GREEN BEANS

Ingredients for 4 servings:

- 1 lb. 5 oz. (600 g.) Beef Stew Meat
- 1 lb. 5 oz. (600 g.) Green Beans
- 1-2 Roma Tomatoes
- 1 medium onion
- 7-8 cloves garlic
- 2-3 tablespoons vegetable oil

Spices: 1 teaspoon paprika, 1 teaspoon crushed red pepper, 2 tablespoons finely chopped parsley, salt to taste.

Way of preparation:

Preheat 2.6 pints (1 ½ liters) of water in a pot. Add a pinch of salt and the cleaned green beans. If they are long cut them into smaller pieces. Leave them on the stove for 10 minutes. Then drain them. Cut the onion into slices and tomatoes - into small pieces. Stew the meat with the onion, whole garlic cloves, paprika, crushed red pepper, oil and a little water for 15 minutes. Add 1 ½ cups of hot water and cook the mixture on low heat for 1 hour. Add the tomatoes, green beans and salt to taste. Cook the dish until the meat softens and the liquid evaporates. Add the parsley and remove the pot from the stove. Serve the dish warm.

Combines with:

Vegetable salads and vegetable soups - without potatoes; to them may be added meat, chicken, ham, mushrooms, olives (prepared according to the recipes of this book).

17.1. OKRA SOUP WITH POTATOES

Ingredients for 4 servings:
- 7 oz. (200 g.) fresh okra
- 7 oz. (200 g.) white potatoes
- 1sweet onion
- 2 cloves garlic
- 2 tablespoons vegetable oil

Spices: 2 tablespoons finely chopped parsley, 1 tablespoon vinegar, 1 teaspoon paprika, ground pepper and salt to taste.

Way of preparation:

Clean the okra and let it stand for 30 minutes in a mixture of 2 cups of cold water, vinegar and salt. Finely chop the onion, garlic and potatoes, stew in the oil. After 3-4 minutes, add the paprika. Stir the mixture well, add 3 - 4 cups of cold water. When it boils put in the okra and salt to taste. Cook the soup for 20-25 minutes. Remove the pot from the stove. Sprinkle the soup with parsley and black pepper.

Serve with: *Vegetable Curry*

17.2. VEGETABLE CURRY

Ingredients for 4 servings:
- 2 green zucchini or yellow squash
- 1 medium eggplant
- 1 lb. (454 g.) potatoes
- 4 oz. (113 g.) green beans
- ½ cup onion, cut into slice
- 4-5 cloves garlic
- 2-3 tablespoons vegetable oil

Spices: 2 teaspoons curry, a pinch of cumin, 1 bay leaf, salt to taste, 1-2 tablespoons finely chopped parsley.

Way of preparation:
Peel the potatoes, zucchini and eggplant and cut them into thin rings. Cut the garlic finely. In a baking tray arrange in layers the eggplants, potatoes and zucchini (or yellow squash). Among the layers sprinkle with the mixture made from green beans, onion, garlic, curry, cumin, bay leaf and salt. Pour them with 1 cup of water and oil. Preheat the oven to 392 F / 200 C. Bake the dish for about 45 minutes. Serve it warm. Sprinkle each serving with parsley.

18.1. FISH SOUP WITH GREEN ONION AND OLIVES

Ingredients for 4 servings:
- 11 oz. (312 g.) Branzino Fillets

- 2-3 green onions
- 1 green pepper and 1 yellow pepper
- 1 Roma Tomato
- 1 tablespoon olive oil
- 8 pitted black olives - cut into quarters

Spices: 1 teaspoon lovage, 2 tablespoons finely chopped parsley, ground black pepper and salt to taste.

Way of preparation:

Heat the olive oil in a pot. Finely chop the onion, peppers and tomato - into small pieces. Put the onion to stew for 2-3 minutes. Then add the peppers, tomatoes, salt and black pepper. After 2-3 minutes, pour the mixture with 4 cups of hot water. Cut the fish into portions. Add it to the vegetables. Leave the soup to cook for 10-15 minutes. Add the olives, parsley and lovage. Remove the soup from the stove. Serve it warm.

Serve with: *Fish Rolls Stuffed with Spinach*

18.2. FISH ROLLS STUFFED WITH SPINACH

Ingredients for 4 servings:

- 4 large fresh fish fillets
- ground black pepper and salt to taste
- 1-2 tablespoons vegetable oil

For the filling: 7 oz. (200 g.) spinach, 1-2 tablespoon oil, a pinch of grated nutmeg, 1 tablespoon lemon, 1 clove crushed garlic, 1 small onion - finely chopped, ground black pepper and salt to taste.

Way of preparation:

Preheat the oven to 428 F / 220 C.

Stew the onion, garlic and spinach in the oil. Sprinkle with salt and add the other products for the filling. Sprinkle the fish fillets with black pepper and salt to taste. Divide the filling into 4 parts and on each fillet spread ¼ part of the filling. Wrap the roll, starting from the thin part of the fish fillet. Arrange the rolls in a greased baking tray. Cover it with aluminum foil. Bake the dish in the oven for 25-30 minutes.

19.1. BBQ: CHICKEN SKEWERS IN BACON

Ingredients for 4 servings:
- 1 lb. 8 oz. (680 g.) Chicken Breasts
- 5 oz. (150 g.) Bacon

For the marinade: 2 tablespoons vegetable oil, the juice of 1 lemon, zest of 1 lemon, 1 tablespoon chopped parsley, ½ tablespoon chopped rosemary 2 sprigs finely chopped green onion.

Way of preparation:
Cut the chicken breasts into the same sized cubes. Put them in a deep bowl with the marinade. Leave them to stand for 2-3 hours in the refrigerator. Stir them occasionally. Drain the chicken pieces, wrap each with thinly cut slices of bacon. Thread them on skewers and grill them for about 10-12 minutes. Turn them on 3-4 minutes and each time brush them with the marinade. Serve them warm.
Serve with: *Vegetable Skewers*

19.2. VEGETABLE SKEWERS

Ingredients for 4 servings:
- 2 medium zucchini
- 12 cherry tomatoes
- 1 head garlic
- 18 green onions
- 12 bay leaves

Spices: 2 tablespoons olive oil, ½ teaspoon thyme, ground black pepper and salt to taste
Way of preparation:
Wash well all the vegetables. Cut the zucchini into thick rings. Peel

the garlic and onions. Prepare skewers as alternately thread zucchini, onion, tomato, garlic, bay leaf. Sprinkle with salt and black pepper. Brush the skewers with olive oil and sprinkle with thyme. Bake them on the grill for 8 minutes, turning them frequently.

20.1. STUFFED EGGPLANTS WITH GROUND BEEF

Ingredients for 4 servings:
- 4 medium eggplants

For the filling: 5 oz. (142 g.) fresh field mushrooms – cut into small pieces, 9 oz. (255 g.) ground beef, 1 onion – finely chopped, 2-3 tablespoons vegetable oil, 2 tablespoons finely chopped parsley, a pinch of thyme, 1 teaspoon paprika, ground black pepper and salt to taste.

Way of preparation:
Wash and peel the eggplants, remove the stalks. Cut them lengthwise into two halves. Using a spoon remove their inner part. Heat the oil in a pan, add the mushrooms, onion and ¼ of the inner part of the eggplants. After 7-8 minutes, add the ground beef, black pepper, paprika and salt to taste. Stir the mixture until the meat is crumbled. Stew the mixture for another 10-15 minutes. Remove the pan from the stove and add the parsley and thyme. Stir the filling.

Fill the curved eggplants. Put them in a baking tray with ½ cup of hot water. Preheat the oven to 392 F / 200 C. Place the tray in the oven and bake the dish for 30-40 minutes. Serve it warm.

Serve with: *"Village" Salad with Turkey Ham*

20.2. "VILLAGE" SALAD WITH TURKEY HAM

Ingredients for 4 servings:
- 3 oz. (85 g.) Turkey Ham
- 4 Cluster Tomatoes
- 1 large cucumber

- 1 small red onion
- 3.5 oz. (100 g.) fresh mushrooms
- 8 - 12 green olives

Spices: 2 tablespoons grapeseed oil, 2 tablespoons finely chopped parsley, salt to taste.

Way of preparation:

Clean the mushrooms and cut them into small cubes. Put the mushrooms with 1 cup of water and a pinch of salt to cook for 10 minutes. Then drain them well and let them cool. Cut into small cubes the tomatoes, cucumber and onion. Put the cut products in a large bowl, stir them carefully. On top distribute the turkey ham, cut into thin strips. Add the olives, sprinkle with parsley, salt and grapeseed oil.

21.1. SHALLOTS WITH MUSHROOMS IN OVEN

Ingredients for 4 servings:

- 11 oz. (312 g.) shallots
- 3.5 oz. (100 g.) fresh field mushrooms
- 1 yellow onion
- 2 sweet red peppers
- 1 cup rice
- 8-12 pitted black olives
- 2-3 tablespoons vegetable oil
- 1/3 cup white wine

Spices: 2 tablespoons finely chopped parsley, ground black pepper and salt to taste.

Way of preparation:

Clean the shallots and leave them whole. Clean the mushrooms and onion and cut them into slices. Cut the peppers into small pieces. Heat the oil and stew the onion for 2 minutes. To them add the cleaned shallots, the olives cut into four lengthwise, mushrooms and black pepper. Pour over the vegetables with the wine. After 4 - 5 minutes, add 2 cups of warm water. Sprinkle the mixture with salt and let it cook on low heat 2 – 3 minutes. Add the rice and peppers. Replace the dish into a baking tray. Preheat the oven to 392 F / 200 C.

Put the tray in the oven. Bake the dish for 20 minutes. Serve it warm. Sprinkle it with parsley.

Serve with: *Vegetable Salad with Fresh Herbs*

21.2. VEGETABLE SALAD WITH FRESH HERBS

Ingredients for 4 servings:
- 14 oz. (400 g.) Cherry Tomatoes
- 1 medium cucumber
- 4 green onion

Spices: 7-8 fresh garden mint leaves, 2 tablespoons finely chopped parsley, 5-6 basil leaves, 1-2 tablespoons olive oil.

Way of preparation:

In the middle of serving plates arrange the cucumber cut into rings. Around them in a circle arrange the tomatoes cut into rings. Sprinkle the cucumbers with the garden mint and tomatoes with parsley and basil. Sprinkle the salad with finely chopped spring onions and olive oil. Serve the salad immediately after its preparation.

22.1. ZUCCHINI SOUP AND FENNEL

Ingredients for 4 servings:
- 2 medium zucchini
- ½ cup fennel
- 7 oz. (200 g.) potatoes
- 1 medium carrot
- 2 cloves garlic
- 1-2 tablespoons vegetable oil

Spices: 2 tablespoons finely chopped parsley, ground black pepper and salt to taste.

Way of preparation:
Peel and cut into small cubes the zucchini, potatoes and carrot. Chop the garlic and fennel finely. Heat the oil and put them to stew for 10 minutes. Stir them occasionally. Add 4 cups of warm water, salt and black pepper. Leave the soup to cook on low heat for 20-25 minutes. Remove the pot from the stove. Sprinkle the soup with parsley and serve it warm.
Serve with: *Potato Skewers with Garlic*

22.2. POTATO SKEWERS WITH GARLIC

Ingredients for 4 servings:
- 24 small potatoes

For the marinade: 2 heads garlic, 6 tablespoons vegetable oil, zest and juice of 1 lemon, 1 tablespoon thyme, 1 teaspoon paprika, ground black pepper and salt to taste.

Way of preparation:
Put the potatoes in a deep pot. Pour them with water enough to cover them. Add 1 teaspoon salt. Put the pot on the stove. Cook the potatoes for 8-10 minutes (be careful not to overcook them, they should remain whole). In a deep bowl, mix the oil, lemon juice and zest, thyme, 4 cloves of finely chopped garlic, paprika, salt and black pepper to taste. Put the peeled warm potatoes in the marinade. Leave them to stand for 1 hour. During this time boil the remaining garlic cloves (without peeling them) in hot water for 5 minutes. Remove them, pour them with cold water and dry them. Prepare skewers of the potatoes and garlic cloves. Bake them on the grill for 10 minutes as turning them and pouring them with the marinade. Potatoes must remain crunchy. Serve them as a main dish.

23.1. SUMMER STEW WITH TURKEY BREASTS

Ingredients for 4 servings:

- 1 lb. 5 oz. (600 g.) Turkey Breast
- 1 yellow onion
- 1 medium carrot
- 1 small eggplant
- 1 small zucchini
- 2 Cubanelle peppers
- ½ cup green beans
- ½ cup fresh okra
- 2 roma tomatoes
- 3 tablespoons vegetable oil

Spices: 3 tablespoons finely chopped parsley, 1 tablespoon ground savory (or oregano), 2 teaspoons paprika, salt to taste.

Way of preparation:

Wash the vegetables, cut them into large pieces. Cut the turkey breast into portions. Stew the meat in the oil. Then put it with all the vegetables and spices in a clay pot or deep pot. Pour with 2 cups of hot water. Cover tightly with the lid the clay pot or the deep pot and put it in the oven (the clay pot) or on the stove (the deep pot). Bake/cook the dish on low heat until the meat softens : 356 F / 180 C. Serve the dish warm, sprinkle it with parsley. The most appropriate side dish is lettuce salad or salad of tomatoes and cucumbers.

Combines with:

Vegetable salads and vegetable soups - without potatoes; to them may be added meat, chicken, ham, mushrooms, olives (prepared according to the recipes of this book).

24.1. COLD ZUCCHINI SOUP WITH CHEESE

Ingredients for 4 servings:

- 1 lb. (454 g.) green zucchini
- 2 cloves garlic
- 1 small sweet onion
- 2 - 3 tablespoons yogurt
- 4 oz. (113 g.) Blue Cheese

Spices: 1 tablespoon finely chopped dill, ground black pepper and salt to taste.

Way of preparation:

Wash, peel and put the zucchini in a deep bowl. Add the finely chopped onion, garlic and the yogurt. Puree the mixture. Add salt and black pepper, 3 ½ cups of cold water and some ice. Leave the soup in the refrigerator for 15 minutes. Then add to each portion crumbled blue cheese and dill. Serve the soup in warm summer days.

<u>**Serve with:**</u> *Stuffed Mushrooms with Melted Cheese*

24.2. STUFFED MUSHROOMS WITH MELTED CHEESE

Ingredients for 4 servings:

- 12 large fresh brown field mushrooms (can be white)

For the filling: ½ tablespoon butter, 12 pieces melted cheese (with the size of a walnut), 2 tomatoes, 2 cloves pressed garlic, salt and ground black pepper to taste, 1 tablespoons basil.

Way of preparation:

Clean the mushrooms thoroughly with a brush. Remove the stems and cut them into small pieces. Finely chop the tomato. In a pan heat ¼ tablespoon of butter. Put in the stems and tomatoes and garlic to stew until the liquid evaporates. Add the melted cheese, basil, black pepper and salt to taste. Stir the filling and remove the pan from the stove. Stuff each mushroom with a part of the filling (do not overfill the mushrooms). Put them in a baking tray. Preheat the oven to 428 F / 220 C. Put the tray in the oven. Bake the stuffed mushrooms for 20-25 minutes until crust. Serve them warm with fresh salad or soup.

25.1. TROUT WITH LEMON FLAVOR

Ingredients for 4 servings:

- 4 whole small trout

- 1 lemon - cut into 4 slices
- 2-3 tablespoons vegetable oil

For the marinade: ½ teaspoon chilli, ground black pepper and salt to taste, 2 cloves pressed garlic, juice of 1 lemon.

Way of preparation:

Clean, wash and dry the fish. Make several notches on both sides of the fish. Prepare the marinade in a small bowl. Mix the chili, black pepper, salt, garlic and the juice of 1 lemon. With this marinade brush each fish from all sides. Leave the fishes in the refrigerator for 1 hour. Then drain the fishes.

Then heat a nonstick pan. Put the oil in it to warm. Place the fishes carefully one to each other in the pan. Put a lid and leave them to stew for 10 minutes. Then turn them and leave them for 6-7 more minutes. Serve the fish hot with a slice of lemon.

Combines with:

Vegetable salads and vegetable soups - without potatoes; to them may be added fish, seafood, fish caviar, mushrooms, olives (prepared according to the recipes of this book).

26.1. BEEF RUMP ROAST WITH AROMATIC SAUCE

Ingredients for 4 servings:

- 25 oz. (708 g.) Beef Rump Roast - whole piece

For the sauce: 2-3 tomatoes, 2 red sweet peppers, 1 sweet onion, 10-12 grains black pepper, 2 tablespoons vegetable oil, 5-6 cloves garlic, 1 bay leaf, 2-3 sprigs fresh thyme, 1 teaspoon coriander, 1 glass of white wine, ground black pepper and salt to taste.

Way of preparation:

Cut all the vegetables into small pieces. Put them together with the spices in a deep baking tray. Rub the meat with ground black pepper. Heat the oil in a pan on low heat. Put in it the whole piece of veal. Leave it on each side for a few minutes until crust. Transfer the meat into the baking tray over the vegetables. Pour over with the wine and ½ cup of hot water. Cover the tray with aluminum foil. Preheat the oven to 338 F / 170 C. Place the tray in the oven for 3 - 4 hours. Then remove the meat and let it cool. Cut it into thin slices. Strain the sauce form the baking through a strainer. Put it on high heat until thickened. Then pour over each serving of cold meat with 1-2 tablespoons of hot sauce.

Serve with: *Stuffed Mushrooms with Dill and Garlic*

26.2. STUFFED MUSHROOMS WITH DILL AND GARLIC

Ingredients for 4 servings:
• 12 large fresh brown field mushrooms (can be white)

For the filling: ½ tablespoon butter, 4 tablespoons finely chopped dill (or other herb), 3 - 4 cloves garlic, salt and ground black pepper to taste.

Way of preparation:
Clean the mushrooms thoroughly with a brush. Remove the stems and cut them into small pieces. Chop finely the dill and garlic. In a pan heat ¼ tablespoon of butter. Put the stems and garlic to stew until the liquid evaporates. Add the dill, black pepper and salt. Stir the mixture and remove the pan from the stove. Stuff each mushroom with some of the filling. Put them in a baking tray. On each mushroom put a little butter. Preheat the oven to 390 F / 200 C. Put the tray in the oven. Bake the stuffed mushrooms for 20-25 minutes until crust. Serve them warm.

27.1. STUFFED TOMATOES WITH GROATS

Ingredients for 4 servings:
• 4 large tomatoes
• 1-2 tablespoons vegetable oil - for sprinkling
• 4 fresh basil leaves - for decoration

For the filling: ¾ cup groats, 2 tablespoons vegetable oil, 2 green onion, 1 small carrot, 1-2 ribs celery, 7-8 basil leaves, ground black pepper and salt to taste.

Way of preparation:

Cut caps of each tomato. Curve the tomatoes with a small spoon. Turn the tomatoes upside down to drain their liquid.

Place the groats in a deep bowl and pour it with 2 cups of hot water. Cover and leave it for 30 minutes to absorb the water. Clean, wash and finely chop the onion, carrot and celery. Heat the oil in a pan. Add the chopped vegetables, 5-6 tablespoons of water and stew them on low heat. Then add the groats, ¼ part of the inner part of the tomatoes, basil, salt and black pepper. Stir the mixture for 3-4 minutes and then remove it from the stove. Stuff the tomatoes with the filling. Put the caps on them and arrange in a baking tray. Sprinkle them with oil. Preheat the oven to 392 F / 200 C. Put the tray in the oven and bake the dish for 20 minutes. Serve one tomato per each portion. Decorate it with basil leaf.

Serve with: *Eggplants with Crunchy Crust*

27.2. EGGPLANT WITH CRUNCHY CRUST

Ingredients for 4 servings:

- 2 eggplants
- 4-5 tablespoons flour
- 4-5 tablespoons breadcrumbs
- 1 tablespoon sesame seeds
- 1 tablespoon sunflower seed
- 5-6 tablespoons vegetable oil

Spices: 3 teaspoons paprika, salt to taste.

Way of preparation:

Preheat the oven to 392 F / 200 C. Wash the eggplants and cut them into 0.4 inches (1 cm.) thick rings. Put them in a bowl and sprinkle with salt. Leave them to stand for 1 hour. Then wash the eggplants with cold water and dry them with kitchen paper. In a shallow plate prepare a dry mixture of flour, bread crumbs, sesame seeds, sunflower seeds, salt and paprika. Take a large shallow baking tray. Smear it with oil. Roll each eggplant ring in the dry mixture. Arrange them in the baking tray so that overlap (such as roof tiles). Sprinkle with oil and place the tray in the oven. Bake them until a crunchy crust. Serve them warm.

28.1. WHITE FISH STEW WITH CAPERS

Ingredients for 4 servings:
- 24 oz. (680 g.) fillet of white fish (or other fish of your choice)
- 1 tablespoon Capers
- 12 – 16 green and black pitted olives
- 2 sweet onions
- 3 tablespoons vegetable oil

Spices: 2 tablespoons finely chopped parsley, 1 – 2 Chili peppers, ground black pepper and salt to taste.

Way of preparation:
Cut the onion into thin slices. Heat the oil in a deep pan. Put the onions with a pinch of salt to stew for 10 minutes on low heat. Then add the chili peppers. Pour the mixture into the pan and add 1/3 cup of water and the white fish fillets. Cook the dish for 10 minutes and add the olives and capers. After 5 minutes, remove the dish from the stove. Sprinkle it with parsley and ground black pepper. Serve the stew of fish warm with fresh vegetable salad.

Combines with:
Vegetable salads and vegetable soups - without potatoes; to them may be added fish, seafood, fish caviar, mushrooms, olives (prepared according to the recipes of this book).

29.1. WHOLEGRAIN PASTA WITH SAUCE

Ingredients for 4 servings:
- 1 lb. (454 g.) pasta of your choice (spaghetti, tagliatelle, pasta, etc.)

For the sauce: 1 lb. (454 g.) tomatoes, 2 red sweet peppers, 2 cloves finely chopped garlic, 10 - 12 pitted black olives, 2 - 3 sprigs fresh basil, 2 - 3 tablespoons olive oil, salt to taste, 1 teaspoon chilli (optional).

Way of preparation:
Peel the tomatoes, cut them into large pieces and put them in a blender. Cut the stems of the peppers. Cut them in half and clean the seeds. Wash them, cut them into pieces and put them together with the tomatoes. Turn the blender on for 10-15 seconds. Add the garlic. Heat the olive oil and put the mixture to stew for 10-15 minutes on low heat. Add the basil, olives and chilli (optional), remove the pan from the stove.
Put in a deep pot 3 ½ pints (2 liters) of cold water. When it starts to boil, add a pinch of salt and the pasta. Cook it following the directions on the package (about 8-10 minutes). Drain the pasta and add it in the sauce. Stir the pasta and serve it hot.

Combines with:
Vegetable salads and vegetable soups - without potatoes; to them may be added croutons, spaghetti, pasta, bread crumbs, flour, bread, mushrooms, olives (prepared according to the recipes of this book).

30.1. CORNISH HEN WITH MUSHROOMS

Ingredients for 8-10 servings:
- 1 Cornish hen about 4½ lbs. (2.040 g.)
- 3 yellow onions
- 7 oz. (200 g.) small fresh mushrooms
- 1½ oz. (40 g.) butter
- 1 tablespoon tomato paste
- 2-3 cloves garlic
- 1 cup white wine

Spices: 1 bay leaf, 2 tablespoons parsley, ½ tablespoon thyme, ground black pepper and salt to taste.

Way of preparation:
Clean the mushrooms. Heat ½ of the butter in a small pan. Put the mushrooms and stew them for 10-15 minutes. Sprinkle with ground black pepper and a pinch of salt. After 2-3 minutes, remove them from the stove.

Cut the hen into portions. Rub the pieces with ground black pepper and salt. Melt in a pan ½ of the butter. Put the hen pieces and cook them for 10-15 minutes. Then cut the onion into slices and add them into the pan. Put a lid on the pan and stew the mixture for another 7-8 minutes. Add the wine and tomato paste dissolved into 1 cup of cold water. Stir well and add the bay leaf, thyme, garlic, black pepper and salt. Let the dish simmer on low heat until the meat softens completely. Then add the mushrooms. Stir and after 5 minutes, remove the dish from the stove. Serve it warm, sprinkle it with parsley.

This dish is suitable for a festive lunch.

Combines with:

Vegetable salads and vegetable soups - without potatoes; to them may be added meat, chicken, ham, mushrooms, olives (prepared according to the recipes of this book).

SUMMER - DINNER

31.1. MARINATED TURKY BREAST CUTLETS ON A PAN

Ingredients for 4 servings:
- 1 lb. 8 oz. (680 g.) Turkey Breast Cutlets
- 1-2 tablespoons oil

For the marinade: 2-3 cloves garlic, 7-8 sprigs parsley, 3-4 sprigs fresh oregano, 2-3 sprigs thyme, 1 teaspoon paprika, a pinch of ground cumin, a pinch of ground black pepper, juice from ½ lemon , ¼ cup white wine, 2 tablespoons oil.

Way of preparation:
Finely chop the garlic, parsley, oregano and thyme. Put them in a deep bowl. Add the juice lemon, wine and oil. Stir the mixture vigorously. Put cutlets in the marinade. Stir and cover the bowl with foil. Leave it in the refrigerator for 12 hours. Then remove the cutlets. Put them in a heated pan with 1-2 tablespoons of oil. After 6-7 minutes, turn them. Leave them for another 5-6 minutes.
<u>**Serve with:**</u> *Salad with Mini Peppers*

31.2. SALAD WITH MINI PEPPERS

Ingredients for 4 servings:
- 1 lettuce
- 3 sweet mini peppers (red, yellow, orange)
- 2 medium tomatoes

Spices: 2 tablespoons olive oil, 4 lemon slices, salt to taste, 5-6 sprigs parsley.

Way of preparation:
Cut the peppers into thin strips. Wash the tomatoes and cut them into 6-8 pieces. Wash the lettuce with cold water. Shred or chop its leaves on large pieces. Spread them on a serving plate. On them evenly place tomatoes and peppers. Sprinkle the salad with olive oil, salt and parsley. Decorate it with lemon slices.

32.1. VEGETABLE STEW WITH RICE

Ingredients for 4 servings:
- 1 cup rice
- 1 yellow onion
- 1 large carrot
- 2 green or red sweet peppers
- 1 cup petite diced tomatoes
- 3 tablespoons vegetable oil

Spices: 2 teaspoons paprika, 2 tablespoons finely chopped parsley, salt to taste.

Way of preparation:
Clean, wash and cut into small pieces the vegetables. Stew in the oil the onion, peppers and carrots. Put the paprika, stir and pour over the steamed vegetables with 2 ½ cups of hot water. When the mixture boils, add the rice and salt to taste. After 10 minutes, add the tomatoes. Let the dish simmer on low heat until the rice softens. Before removing the dish, add the parsley, stir it well. Remove the pot from the stove. Leave the pot with a lid for 15 minutes (so the rice will absorb all the water).

Serve with: Salad of Roasted Sweet Peppers

32.2. SALAD OF ROASTED SWEET PEPPERS

Ingredients for 4 servings:
- 6 red sweet peppers
- 6 green sweet peppers

Spices: 2 - 3 tablespoons finely chopped parsley.

For the dressing: 2 tablespoons olive oil, ½ tablespoon vinegar, 1-2 cloves crushed garlic, salt to taste.

Way of preparation:
Bake the peppers on a grill, in the oven or on the stove. Put them in a bag. When cool, peel them. Cut the stalks and clean them from the seeds. Cut the peppers into long strips. Arrange them in a

serving plate, alternating colors. Prepare the dressing from the olive oil, vinegar, garlic and salt. Pour the roasted peppers with the dressing and sprinkle with parsley.

33.1. PORK BACK RIBS ON GRILL

Ingredients for 4 servings:
- 4 lbs. (1.820 g.) Pork Loin Back Ribs

For the marinade: 1 onion - finely chopped, 2 tablespoons tomato paste, 4-5 tablespoons soy sauce, 1 coffee cup vegetable oil, 2 tablespoons vinegar, 1 chili - cleaned of the seeds and cut in two, ground black pepper.

Way of preparation:
Put in a deep bowl all the ingredients for the marinade. Mix them vigorously.

Put the ribs in a large pot with boiling salted water. Let them cook on low heat for 30 - 40 minutes. Then drain them, leave them to cool. Cut them into small pieces. Put them in the prepared marinade, pour them everywhere. Leave them to stand for 1 hour in the refrigerator. Turn them occasionally. Then drain them well, put them to bake on the grill for 5 minutes on each side. Serve the ribs warm.

Serve with: *Salad with Zucchini (Or Yellow Squash)*

33.2. SALAD WITH ZUCCHINI (or YELLOW SQUASH)

Ingredients for 4 servings:
- 1 lb. (454 g.) Zucchini or Yellow Squash
- 2 red tomatoes

Spices: juice from ½ lemon, 2 tablespoons olive oil, 6-7 leaves fresh basil, 4-5 sprigs fresh dill, salt to taste.

Way of preparation:
Peel the zucchini and cut them into thin rings. Put them in hot water for 2-3 minutes. Drain them of the water and leave them to cool. Cut the tomatoes into cubes and add them to the zucchini.

Pour the salad with olive oil, lemon juice. Cover the salad with foil and put it in the refrigerator for 15 minutes. Serve it decorated with sprigs of dill and basil. Sprinkle it with salt and before eating.

34.1.FISH FILLET WITH ASPARAGUS ON GRILL

Ingredients for 4 servings:
- 1 lb.10 oz. (737 g.) Tilapia Fillets
- 5 oz. (142 g.) fresh asparagus

For dressing: 2-3 tablespoons olive oil, juice from ½ lemon, 1 teaspoon pasted garlic, ground black pepper and salt to taste.

Way of preparation:
Sprinkle the fish fillets with black pepper and salt. Place asparagus on each fillet. Turn in into roll. Bake on the grill for 5 - 6 minutes on each side. Serve the fish hot. Flush it with dressing from: olive oil, lemon juice, pasted garlic, ground black pepper and salt to taste.

Serve with: *Tomato Salad with Tuna*

34.2. TOMATO SALAD WITH TUNA

Ingredients for 4 servings:
- 2 - 3 tomatoes
- 3 oz. (85 g.) canned tuna in olive oil
- 1 small red onion
- juice from ½ lemon
- 2 tablespoons finely chopped chives feathers
- 4 lettuce leaves

Spices: salt to taste, 8-12 black olives, 4 lemon slices.

Way of preparation:
Wash the tomatoes in cold water and dry them. Cut tomatoes into small cubes. Mix in a bowl the tomatoes, tuna with olive oil, finely chopped onion and feathers chives, lemon juice and salt to taste. Arrange the salad on the leaves of lettuce. Garnish with lemon

slices and olives.

35.1. MEDALLIONS OF EGGPLANT WITH CHEESE

Ingredients for 4 servings:
- 2 large eggplants
- 4 tomatoes
- 2 cloves garlic
- 1 onion
- 4 oz. (113 g.) Cheddar Cheese (or cheese of your choice)
- 3 tablespoons vegetable oil

Spices: 1 teaspoon finely chopped fresh oregano, 2-3 tablespoons finely chopped parsley, ground black pepper and salt to taste.

Way of preparation:
Preheat the oven to 392 F / 200 C.
Finely chop the onion, garlic and tomatoes. In a heavy-bottomed pan heat the oil and put to stew the onion first, and then garlic and tomatoes. Add the parsley, black pepper and a little salt. Leave the sauce on low heat for 10-15 minutes. During this time, wash and peel the eggplants, remove the stalks. Cut them into rings of uniform thickness of about 0.4 inches (1 cm.). Sprinkle with salt and let them to stand for 30 minutes. Then wash them thoroughly with cold water and dry them. Brush them with oil. Preheat a grill pan and bake them for 5 minutes on each side. Arrange the eggplants in a large baking tray. Cover each slice of eggplant with tomato sauce. Over it place a piece of cheese. Put the tray in the oven. Bake the dish for 20-30 minutes. Divide the medallions in serving plates. Pour the sauce of the baking on the side and sprinkle with oregano.
<u>Serve with:</u> *Tomatoes with Mozzarella*

35.2. TOMATOES WITH MOZZARELLA

Ingredients for 4 servings:
- 4 medium tomatoes

- 4 oz. (113 g.) fresh cheese "Mozzarella"

Spices: 1-2 tablespoons of olive oil, 10-12 fresh basil leaves, 4 black olives, black pepper and salt to taste.

Way of preparation:

Wash the tomatoes well. On board with a sharp knife make 4-5 incisions on each tomato without going to the end. Cut the cheese (must be cold from the refrigerator) into thin slices - the number is equal to cuts of tomatoes. Each piece of cheese smear with olive oil, sprinkle it with black pepper and put it in the slot of tomatoes. Sprinkle with basil leaves and olive oil. Leave the tomatoes for 15 minutes in the refrigerator. Serve each portion decorated with olive.

36.1. COUNTRY STYLE BEEF WITH GARLIC

Ingredients for 4 servings:

- 1 lb. 10 oz. (737 g.) Boneless Beef Stew Meat
- 3 yellow onions
- 2 heads garlic
- 3 medium tomatoes
- 1 tablespoon tomato paste
- 2-3 tablespoons vegetable oil

Spices: 1 tablespoon apple cider vinegar, 2 tablespoons finely chopped parsley, ground black pepper and salt to taste.

Way of preparation:

Peel and chop the tomatoes into small pieces. Cut the onions and garlic into thin slices. At the bottom of a pot spread on layers the products as follows: onions, tomatoes on it, on them the meat, on the top the whole garlic cloves. Pour with 2 cups of warm water in which you have dissolved the tomato paste. Add the oil and vinegar, sprinkle with black pepper and salt to taste. Let the dish simmer on low heat for at least 1 hour and 30 minutes to soften the meat. If necessary pour a little more water. Serve the dish warm, sprinkle it with parsley. This dish can be cooked in a pressure cooker.

Combines with:
Vegetable salads and vegetable soups - without potatoes; to them may be added meat, chicken, ham, mushrooms, olives (prepared according to the recipes of this book).

37.1. STUFFED PEPPERS IN AUSTRALIAN STYLE

Ingredients for 4 servings:
- 20 oz. (567 g.) Ground Lamb
- 4-8 Colored Bell Peppers
- cloves finely chopped garlic
- 1 sweet onion
- 3 - 4 tablespoons vegetable oil

Spices: 1 teaspoon ground cumin, 2 sprigs fresh coriander, ground black pepper and salt to taste.

Way of preparation:
Preheat the oven to 390 F / 200 C.

Cut caps of the peppers and clean the seeds. Wash them with cold water. Peel and finely chop the onion. Stew it with 2 tablespoons of oil. Add the lamb, garlic, black pepper and salt to taste. Pour with a little of warm water and continue stewing for 15 minutes. Stir the mixture, the meat must be broken down into very small pieces. Remove the mixture from the stove. Add the coriander and cumin. Stir the mixture well and fill the peppers with the mixture. Put them in a baking tray. Sprinkle with salt and pour them with the remaining oil (you can add a little of warm water). Put the tray in the oven. Bake the peppers for 30 minutes. Serve them warm.

This dish is suitable for Sunday lunch.

Combines with:
Vegetable salads and vegetable soups - without potatoes; to them may be added meat, chicken, ham, mushrooms, olives (prepared according to the recipes of this book).

38.1. "GARDEN" SOUP

Ingredients for 4 servings:
- 14 oz. (414 g.) white potatoes
- 1 medium carrot
- 1 red sweet pepper
- 1 - 2 ribs celery
- 5 oz. (150 g.) green beans
- 1 yellow onion
- 1-2 parsley roots
- 1 parsnip roots
- 2 tablespoons oil

Spices: 2 tablespoons finely chopped parsley, ground black pepper and salt to taste.

Way of preparation:

Heat the oil in a deep pot. Peel, wash and cut into small cubes all the ingredients. Put them to stew for 7-8 minutes with salt, black pepper and a little hot water. Stir the mixture. Then add 4 - 5 cups of warm water. Cook the soup for 30-35 minutes. Before removing it from the stove put in the parsley and stir. Serve the soup warm.

<u>Serve with:</u> Eggplants Stuffed with Walnut Filling

38.2. EGGPLANTS WITH WALNUT FILLING

Ingredients for 4 servings:
- 2 large eggplants - 2 lbs. (907 g.)
- 2 tablespoons vegetable oil
- 1-2 potatoes

For the filling: 3-4 onions, 3 oz. (85 g.) ground walnuts, 2 tablespoons vegetable oil, 2 tablespoons finely chopped parsley, 1 bay leaf, ground black pepper and salt to taste.

Way of preparation:

Wash the eggplants well and remove their stalks. Cut them into two halves along the length. Carve the eggplants, salt them and let them drain. Then wash them with cold water and dry them.

Chop finely ¼ of the carved part of the eggplants and the onions. Put them to stew with 2 tablespoons of oil. After 10 minutes, add the walnuts, parsley, bay leaf, black pepper and salt to taste. Stew the mixture on low heat until the liquid evaporates. Fill the curved eggplants with the walnut filling. Grate potatoes over them.
Arrange them in a baking tray. Preheat the oven to 392 F / 200 C. Put the eggplants to bake until golden brown (about 30 minutes).

39.1. FISH SKEWERS (SALMON)

Ingredients for 4 servings:
- 1 lb. 10 oz. (737 g.) Salmon Fillets (or other meaty fish)
- 2 onions - cut into thick slices
- 12 - 16 Cherry Tomatoes
- 5 - 6 chili peppers

Spices: 1 tablespoon finely chopped parsley, salt to taste.
Way of preparation:
Cut the fish fillets into pieces for skewers. Salt them and thread them on skewers as putting between them pieces of onion, cherry tomato and chili peppers (whole). Place them on a preheated grill. Bake on each side for 5-6 minutes. After baking the fish, serve it warm. Sprinkle skewers with parsley.
Serve with: *Roasted Sweet Peppers with Sauce*

39.2. ROASTED SWEET PEPPERS WITH SAUCE

Ingredients for 4 servings:
- 8-12 green or red sweet peppers

For the tomato sauce: 24 oz. (680 g.) ripe tomatoes, 2 finely chopped garlic cloves, 2 tablespoons vegetable oil, salt to taste, 2 tablespoons finely chopped parsley.
Way of preparation:
Bake the peppers on a grill, on a stove or in the oven. Right after baking put them in a bag. Leave them until cool. Then peel them, clean the seeds and stalks. Arrange them in a large deep bowl, salt

them lightly.

Peel the tomatoes. Cut them into very small pieces. Heat the oil in a deep pan. Add the tomatoes, garlic and salt to taste. Leave them on the stove without lid, occasionally stir the mixture. Remove the sauce from the heat when thickened. Add to it the parsley. Pour the peppers with the warm sauce. This garnish can be served as warm and cold.

40.1. STUFFED PEPPERS WITH COTTAGE CHEESE

Ingredients for 4 servings:

- 8 Red Bell Peppers

For the filling: 11 oz. (312 g.) cottage cheese and 2-3 tablespoons finely chopped parsley.

For the tomato sauce: 3 ripe tomatoes, 1-2 cloves garlic, 2 tablespoons vegetable oil, 2 tablespoons finely chopped parsley (or basil), salt to taste.

Way of preparation:

Bake the peppers on a grill, stove or in the oven. Put them in a bag for 15-20 minutes. Then peel them, clean them from the seeds and stalks. Salt them lightly and fill them with cottage cheese mixed with parsley. Arrange the peppers in a greased with olive oil baking tray.

Cut the tomatoes into small pieces. Heat the oil in a pan. Put in it the finely chopped garlic and tomatoes. Cook them for 5-6 minutes on medium heat. Add the parsley (basil) and salt. Stir and pour over the peppers with the tomato sauce. Preheat the oven to 392 F / 200 C. Put the tray in the oven. Bake the dish for 20 minutes.

Serve with: *Salad with „Feta" Cheese*

40.2. SALAD WITH „FETA" CHEESE

Ingredients for 4 servings:

- 1- 2 salad tomatoes
- 1 large cucumbers

- 1 sweet onion
- 1 green pepper
- 4 oz. (113 g.) grated "Feta" cheese
- 4 chili peppers

Spices: 2 tablespoons olive oil, 10-15 sprigs parsley.

Way of preparation:

Put in a large bowl the chopped into small cubes tomato, cucumbers and green pepper, finely chopped onion and parsley. Stir gently. Divide the mixture into serving plates, forming salads in the form of a pile. Sprinkle with olive oil and grated cheese. Add 1 chili on top of each pile. Serve the salads immediately after their preparation.

41.1. OVEN-BAKED ZUCCHINI WITH EGGS

Ingredients for 4 servings:

- 2 lbs. (907 g.) zucchini
- 6 large eggs
- 2 cloves pressed garlic
- 4 tablespoons vegetable oil

Spices: 2-3 tablespoons finely chopped parsley, salt to taste

Way of preparation:

Peel and cut the zucchini into rings - about 0.4 inches (1 cm.) thick. Salt them and leave to stand for 30 minutes. Then dry them. Preheat the oven to 392 F / 200 C. Arrange the zucchini on a baking tray smeared, first with garlic then with 1 tablespoon of oil. Put the tray in the oven. Bake the zucchini for about 20 minutes. Beat the eggs well with a pinch of salt, the rest of the oil and parsley. Pour over the zucchini with this mixture and return the tray in the oven. Bake the dish, until browned. Serve it warm.

<u>Serve with:</u> *Salad with Mayonnaise Sauce*

41.2. SALAD WITH MAYONNAISE SAUCE

Ingredients for 4 servings:

- 2 bunch Purslane
- 2 large cucumbers
- 4 green onion
- 8 - 10 pitted olives

Spices: 10 sprigs parsley, 7-8 leaves fresh garden mint.

For the sauce: 1 cup mayonnaise, 2 cloves crushed garlic.

Way of preparation:

Cut the cucumbers and onion into small cubes. Cut the olives into 5-6 pieces. Finely chop the purslane, parsley and garden mint. Put the cut products in a large bowl. Separately prepare the sauce from the mayonnaise and crushed garlic. Serve the salad and sauce separately.

42.1. TOMATO SOUP WITH CHICKEN

Ingredients for servings:
- 1 lb. (454 g.) Chicken Quarters
- 1 yellow onion
- 1 teaspoon butter or
- 8 oz. (227 g.) tomatoes

Spices: 2 tablespoons chopped fresh parsley, ground black pepper and salt to taste.

Way of preparation:

Cut the onion finely. Peel and grate the tomatoes coarsely. Melt the butter in a deep pot. Stew the onion, add the chicken cut into pieces. Pour the mixture with 5 cup water. After 30 minutes, remove the chicken with a slotted spoon. Remove the bones and put the chicken back in the broth. Add the tomatoes, black pepper and salt to taste. Cook the soup for 10 minutes. Remove the pot from the stove. Add parsley and serve the soup warm.

Serve with: *Fresh Salad with Sesame Seed and Ham*

42.2. FRESH SALAD WITH SESAME SEED AND HAM

Ingredients for 4 servings:

- 4 oz. (113 g.) cooked ham
- 1 tablespoon sesame seeds
- 4 lettuce leaves
- 1 salad tomato
- 1 large cucumber
- 1 Cubanelle green pepper
- 1 cubanelle red pepper
- 1 large carrot
- 1 small onion
- 1 tablespoon finely chopped parsley

For the dressing: 3-4 tablespoons vegetable oil, 1 tablespoon vinegar, 1 teaspoon mustard, 1 small onion - grated, ground black pepper and salt to taste.

Way of preparation:
Prepare the dressing in a deep bowl. Put all the ingredients and mix them vigorously. Let it stand in a refrigerator for about 10 minutes. Peel and grate the carrot. In each serving plate put a lettuce leaf. On it arrange piles of the various types of chopped vegetables into small cubes, grated carrot and ham. Sprinkle with the finely chopped onion, sesame seeds and parsley. Pour the prepared salad with the dressing. Serve it immediately after its preparation.

43.1. PORK WITH RED WINE AND MUSHROOMS

Ingredients for 4 servings:
- 21 oz. (600 g.) Boneless Pork Stew Meat
- ½ cup red wine
- 2 yellow onions
- 6 oz. (170 g.) fresh field mushrooms
- 3 tablespoons vegetable oil

Spices: 1 - 2 teaspoons paprika, 10 - 12 grains black pepper, 1 - 2 bay leaves, salt to taste, a pinch of ground black pepper.

Way of preparation:
Clean the mushrooms and cut them into quarters. Heat 1

tablespoon of oil in a pan. Put the mushrooms for 3-4 minutes, do not stir them. Sprinkle with ground black pepper and a pinch of salt. Leave them for another 3-4 minutes on the stove, then remove them.

Cut the onion very finely. Wash and dry the pork. Heat 2 tablespoons of oil in a pot and put the onions and meat to stew. After 10 minutes, add the paprika and stir. Pour the wine, add the black pepper grains and bay leaf. Stir and leave the dish on low heat for 10 minutes. Then pour 1- 1½ cups of hot water. Put the lid and cook the dish on low heat for 1-1 ½ hours. Before you remove it from the stove, add the mushrooms. If necessary add salt and serve the dish warm.

Combines with:

Vegetable salads and vegetable soups - without potatoes; to them may be added meat, chicken, ham, mushrooms, olives (prepared according to the recipes of this book).

44.1. SPICY SEAFOOD SOUP

Ingredients for 4 servings:
- 4 oz. (113 g.) prawns
- 12 cleaned mussels
- 7 oz. (200 g.) fillet Tilapia (or other fish)
- 1-2 cloves garlic
- 1 crushed red pepper
- 1 tablespoon grated onion
- juice from ½ lemon

Spices: 1 teaspoon grated ginger, 5-6 finely chopped fresh coriander, ground black pepper and salt to taste.

Way of preparation:

Cut the fish into portions. Wash the prawns. Put in a pot 4 cups of water. When the water boils, add the salt, fish, garlic, crushed red pepper, black pepper, onion, ginger and salt to taste. After 5-6 minutes, add the mussels and prawns. Let them cook for 7-8 minutes. Remove the pot from the stove and add the juice from ½ lemon and the coriander. Serve the soup warm, sprinkle it with coriander.

Serve with: *Zucchini with Vegetables in Oven*

44.2. ZUCCHINI WITH VEGETABLES IN OVEN

Ingredients for 4 servings:
- 28 oz. (800 g.) zucchini
- 2-3 yellow onions
- 2-3 sweet green or red peppers
- 2 medium carrots
- 4-5 cloves garlic
- 2-3 roma tomatoes
- ½ lemon
- 4 tablespoons vegetable oil

Spices: 1 bay leaf, 10-12 sprigs finely chopped parsley, ground black pepper and salt to taste.

Way of preparation:
Cut the zucchini and tomatoes into rings with a thickness of 0.6 inches (1.5 cm.). Cut the onions into slices, peppers - into pieces, lemon – into slices, carrots - into thin rings.

Arrange in a small baking tray half of the zucchini. Distribute evenly over them a mixture of: onions, peppers, carrots, parsley, garlic, black pepper and a pinch of salt. Over it arrange the remaining zucchini. Cover them with the tomatoes and lemon. Pour the dish with oil and ½ cup of water. Preheat the oven to 392 F / 200 C. Put the dish to bake for 30 minutes. The finished dish should be left without water. Serve it warm.

45.1. TOMATOES AND MAYONNAISE IN AN OVEN

Ingredients for 4 servings:
- 4 large tomatoes - 2 lbs. 10 oz. (1.190 g.)

For the filling: 5 oz. (150 g.) fresh spinach, 1 small sweet onion, 5-6 field mushrooms, 1-2 teaspoons butter, 1 tablespoon finely chopped parsley, 1 tablespoon finely chopped dill, 2 tablespoons mayonnaise, 1 teaspoon mustard, ground black pepper and salt to taste.

Way of preparation:

Cut the mushrooms and onion into small cubes. Mix and stew the vegetables in butter for 5 minutes. Add the parsley and dill. Cut tomatoes into two halves, carve them with a small spoon. Place them upside down for a few minutes to drain. Fill the tomatoes with the vegetable mixture. Thoroughly mix the mayonnaise, mustard, black pepper and salt to taste. Pour each tomato with this mixture. Preheat the oven to 392 F / 200 C. Arrange the tomatoes in a baking tray. Put the tray in the oven and bake the dish for 20-25 minutes.

Combines with:

Vegetable salads and vegetable soups - without potatoes; to them may be added eggs, mushrooms, olives (prepared according to the recipes of this book).

46.1. MUTTON WITH OKRA

Ingredients for 4 servings:
- 21 oz. (600 g.) Mutton (or Beef Stew Meat)
- 21 oz. (600 g.) fresh okra
- 1 sweet onion
- 2-3 roma tomatoes
- 3 - 4 tablespoons vegetable oil

Spices: 2 tablespoons vinegar, 2 teaspoons paprika, salt to taste, 2 sprigs fresh basil.

Way of preparation:

Clean the okra. Put in a deep pot 2.6 pints (1½ liters) of hot water with 1 teaspoon salt and the vinegar. Add the okra. After 6-7 minutes, remove the okra from the water and drain it well. Cut the onion finely and grate the tomatoes coarsely.

Cut the meat into portions. In a pot heat 2 tablespoons of oil. Put the meat to stew for 10 minutes. Pour it with 2 cups of hot water.

Cook until it begins to soften. In a separate pot stew the onions and tomatoes in the remaining oil for 5-6 minutes. Sprinkle with paprika and add the okra. Stir them and add to them the meat. Cook the dish on low heat until the meat softens completely. Serve the dish warm. Sprinkle it with basil.

Combines with:

Vegetable salads and vegetable soups - without potatoes; to them may be added meat, chicken, ham, mushrooms, olives (prepared according to the recipes of this book).

47.1. BBQ: SPICY VEAL SKEWERS

Ingredients for 4 servings:
- 1 lb. 10 oz. (737 g.) boneless veal
- salt to taste

For the marinade: juice of 1 lemon, ½ cup dry white wine, 1 tablespoon curry powder, 4 tablespoons vegetable oil, ground black pepper.

Way of preparation:

Wash the meat with cold water. Dry it with kitchen paper. Cut it into cubes of equal size. In a suitable container stir the oil, wine, lemon juice, curry powder and a pinch of ground black pepper. Pour the meat with this marinade and let it stand in a cool place for 3 - 4 hours. During this time, stir it 3-4 times. Drain the meat pieces. Thread them on skewers. Bake them on not very strong embers for about 30 minutes. Turn them on every 5 minutes and each time brush them with the marinade. Salt them at the end of baking.

Serve with: *BBQ: Mushrooms with Thyme*

47.2. BBQ: MUSHROOMS WITH THYME

Ingredients for 4 servings:
- 1 lb. (454 g.) large fresh field mushrooms
- ½ tablespoon melted butter

- juice of 1 lemon

Spices: 1-2 sprigs fresh thyme, 2 cloves crushed garlic, 1 tablespoon finely chopped parsley, ground black pepper, salt to taste.

Way of preparation:

Clean the mushrooms. Remove the stems. Make several large notches in the caps and pour them with the butter. Sprinkle them with black pepper and salt to taste. Leave them to stand for 5 minutes in the refrigerator. Prepare a mixture of chopped stems and the spices. Fill the mushrooms with this mixture. Place them on a preheated grill and bake for 10 minutes. Roasted mushrooms arrange on a plate, pour them with lemon juice and serve them warm with skewers.

48.1. ZUCCHINI WITH MOZZARELLA CHEESE

Ingredients for 4 servings:

- 3 lbs. (1.350 g.) green zucchini
- 7 oz. (200 g.) Grated Mozzarella Cheese
- 4 tablespoons vegetable oil

Spices: 2 tablespoons finely chopped dill, ground black pepper and salt to taste.

Way of preparation:

Peel and cut the zucchini into rings with thickness of about 0.8 inch (2 cm.). Grease a grill pan with a little oil. Bake the zucchini on both sides. Arrange one half of the zucchini in an oiled small baking tray. Sprinkle with dill, ½ of the cheese and black pepper. Then arrange the remaining zucchini. Sprinkle them with the remaining cheese. Pour them with oil. Preheat the oven to 392 F / 200 C. Put the tray in the oven. Bake the dish for 20 minutes. Serve it warm.

Serve with: *Oak Leaf Salad, Tomato and Cheese*

48.2. OAK LEAF SALAD, TOMATO AND CHEESE

Ingredients for 4 servings:
- 1 "Oak leaf" salad
- 1 salad tomato
- 3.5 oz. (100 g.) Qoat cheese (or Feta cheese)
- 2 green onion
- 10 sprigs parsley

For the dressing: 3 tablespoons olive oil, 2 tablespoons apple vinegar.

Way of preparation:
Wash the vegetables thoroughly with water. Dry the leaves of the "Oak leaf" salad. Shred the leaves into large pieces. Cut the tomato into slices. Finely chop the parsley and onion. Put the vegetables in a large bowl. Pour with the dressing of olive oil and vinegar. Cut the cheese into cubes and distribute it over the vegetables. Serve the salad immediately.

49.1. TURKEY CUTLETS WITH BACON

Ingredients for 4 servings:
- 4 Turkey Breast Cutlets
- 7 oz. (200 g.) bacon
- 1 onion
- ½ cup dry white wine
- 2-3 tablespoons vegetable oil
- 2 oz. (50 g.) coarsely crushed walnuts

Spices: 1 sprig rosemary, ground black pepper and salt to taste.

Way of preparation:
Preheat the oven to 392 F / 200 C.
Cut the bacon into very thin strips. Peel the onion and cut it into slices. Wash the turkey breasts, dry them and sprinkle with black pepper. Put them in a deep baking tray. Over them place the strips of bacon - tightly to each other. Pour over with the wine and 1-2 tablespoons vegetable oil. Cover the baking tray with aluminum foil and put it in the oven. After 10-12 minutes, remove the foil.

Add into the tray the onions, walnuts, rosemary sprig. Sprinkle with salt and black pepper (if necessary add a little warm water). Bake the dish as turkey meat softens completely. Serve the dish warm.

Serve with: *Green Bean Garnish*

49.2. GREEN BEAN GARNISH

Ingredients for 4 servings:
- 12 oz. (340 g.) green beans

For the sauce: 1 tomato – cut into small pieces, 1 onion - finely chopped, 2 ribs celery – finely chopped, 2 tablespoons vegetable oil, 2 tablespoons finely chopped parsley, salt to taste.

Way of preparation:
Clean and wash the green beans with cold water. Boil them in water with a pinch salt. Then drain them well. Heat the oil in a deep pan. Put the onion and tomatoes, celery and a pinch of salt. Stew the mixture for 10-15 minutes. Puree the vegetables until a smooth sauce becomes. Serve the green beans warm, pour them with the sauce. Sprinkle each portion with parsley.

50.1. SALMON BURGERS IN SPICY SAUCE

Ingredients for 4 servings:
For the burgers: 1 lb. 8 oz. (680 g.) skinless salmon fillet (or fillet from other meaty fish), 2 green onions, 2 tablespoons finely chopped parsley, 2 tablespoons finely chopped coriander, ground black pepper and salt to taste.

For the sauce: 2 tablespoons olive oil, 1 lb. (454 g.) tomatoes - peeled and cut into very small pieces, 1 sweet onion - finely chopped, 2 cloves finely chopped garlic, 1 teaspoon paprika, ½ teaspoon ground cumin, ½ teaspoon cayenne pepper.

Way of preparation:
For the burgers: Cut the fillets into pieces. Put them in a blender. Add the spring onions, parsley, coriander, salt and ground black

pepper. Turn on the blender for 10 seconds. Remove the mixture. Grease your hands with olive oil, shape burgers as big as a large walnut. Arrange them in a flat plate or tray and leave them to stand in the refrigerator for 1 hour.

For the sauce: Heat the olive oil in a deep pan. Add the onion and stew it for 5 minutes. Then add the garlic and spices. Stew them on low heat for 1 minute. Put the tomatoes and ½ - 1 cup of hot water. When the mixture starts to boil, reduce the heat. Leave the sauce to simmer on low heat for 15 minutes. Increase the heat and add the fish burgers one by one. Put a lid on the pan and cook for 10 - 12 minutes. Serve the dish warm.

Serve with: *Cucumber Salad with Shrimps*

50.2. CUCUMBER SALAD WITH SHRIMPS

Ingredients for 4 servings:
- 2-3 medium cucumbers
- 4 oz. (113 g.) boiled shrimps
- 12 pitted olives
- 2 cloves crushed garlic

Spices: 5 sprigs dill, ground black pepper and salt to taste.

Way of preparation:
Cut the cucumber into rings, sprinkle them with salt. Prepare a mixture of shrimps, chopped olives, crushed garlic, finely chopped dill and black pepper. Put the mixture over the cucumbers. Serve the salad immediately.

51.1. WHITE BEANS CREAM SOUP

Ingredients for 4 servings:
- 1 cup white beans
- 1 yellow onion
- 1 large carrot
- 1 green pepper
- 1 red pepper

- 2 cloves garlic
- 2 tablespoons vegetable oil

Spices: 2 teaspoons paprika, 2-3 sprigs finely cut fresh garden mint, 1 tablespoon finely cut parsley and salt to taste.

Way of preparation:

Wash the beans and put them in a pressure cooker. Clean, wash and cut into small pieces all the vegetables (onion, carrot, green pepper, red pepper, garlic). Put them in the cooker. Pour the products with 4 - 5 cups of cold water. Add the paprika and the oil. Close carefully the cooker with the lid. Put it on the lowest power of the stove. After the soup boils, leave it to cook for ½ hour on low heat. When the cooker cools, remove the lid. Puree the soup. Add salt, garden mint and parsley. Serve the soup warm.

If you don't have a pressure cooker, put the soup to boil on low heat in a deep pot for 2 hours.

Serve with: *Vegan Dish with Okra*

51.2. VEGAN DISH WITH OKRA

Ingredients for 4 servings:

- 1 lb. 10 oz. (737 g.) okra
- 1 sweet onion
- 14 oz. (414 g.) fresh tomatoes
- 1 medium carrot
- 2 tablespoons vegetable oil

Spices: 1 teaspoon curry, salt to taste, 2 tablespoons finely chopped parsley.

Way of preparation:

Clean the okra. Cut the stalks. Grate the tomatoes. Pour the okra with the grated tomatoes, leave the mixture to stand for half an hour. In a separate pot heat the oil. Finely chop the onion and carrot. Put them to stew with a little water. After 10 minutes, add the curry, okra with tomatoes and salt to taste. Pour ½ cup of hot water. Cook the dish on low heat for 15 minutes. Serve it warm. Sprinkle each portion with parsley.

52.1. MUSHROOM STEW

Ingredients for 4 servings:
- 1 lb. 8 oz. (680 g.) fresh field mushrooms (or other mushrooms of your choice)
- 2 yellow onions
- 2 ripe tomatoes
- 2 cloves garlic
- 2-3 tablespoons vegetable oil

Spices: 2 tablespoons finely chopped dill, ¼ teaspoon ground coriander, ground black pepper and salt to taste

Way of preparation:
Clean and slice the mushrooms on large pieces. Cut the onion into thin rings. Finely chop the garlic and tomatoes. Stew the mushrooms with the oil in a pan with a lid. Once released water, add the onions. When it softens add the tomatoes, garlic, coriander, black pepper and salt. Cook the dish on low heat until the liquid evaporates. Sprinkle the dish with dill.

<u>**Serve with:**</u> *Baby Spinach Salad with Blue Cheese*

52.2. BABY SPINACH SALAD WITH BLUE CHEESE

Ingredients for 4 servings:
- 1 Iceberg Lettuce
- 5 oz. (142 g.) fresh Baby Spinach
- 4 oz. (113 g.) Blue Cheese
- 1 tablespoon walnuts
- 2 green onion for decoration (optional)

For the dressing: 1 tablespoon apple vinegar, 2 tablespoons olive oil, 1 small grated red onion, salt to taste.

Way of preparation:
Wash the spinach and iceberg lettuce thoroughly with cold water and dry it. Cut them in large pieces, put them in a large bowl. Crumble the cheese and mix it with the crushed (in large pieces) walnuts. Sprinkle the spinach and iceberg lettuce with this

mixture. In a separate bowl, prepare the dressing from the olive oil, vinegar, onion, salt and black pepper. Pour the salad with this dressing and serve it immediately. You can decorate it with several sprigs of green onion (optional).

53.1. RIBEYE STEAK WITH MUSTARD

Ingredients for 4 servings:
- 4 Ribeye Steak

Spices: ground black pepper and salt to taste, 1 tablespoon mustard, butter for greasing the grill.

Way of preparation:
Sprinkle the cutlets with black pepper and smear them with mustard. Put them on the grill. Turn the cutlets every 5 - 6 minutes on each side as greasing the grill with butter. Remove the roasted cutlets from the grill and leave them for 10-15 minutes on a board. Then sprinkle them with salt to taste and serve them with vegetable salad.

Combines with:
Vegetable salads and vegetable soups - without potatoes; to them may be added meat, chicken, ham, mushrooms, olives (prepared according to the recipes of this book).

54.1. STUFFED CALAMARI WITH FRESH SPINACH

Ingredients for 4 servings:
- 4 large calamari with tentacles
- 2 teaspoons olive oil

For the filling: 3 - 4 handfuls of fresh spinach, 2 cloves garlic, 1 teaspoon butter, 1 tablespoon minced walnuts salt and ground black pepper to taste, a pinch of grated nutmeg, 2 sprigs fresh thyme.

Way of preparation:
Select hard calamari with spots on the skin. Pull the head of the calamari, then pull the cartilage from the back side. Remove the

innards. Wash the calamari thoroughly with cold water. So the tubes are ready for filling.

For the filling: Cut the heads and tentacles finely. Warm the butter in a pan. In it fry the garlic, chopped spinach, chopped tentacles and heads of the calamari, minced walnuts (hazelnuts), salt, black pepper and nutmeg. Stir the mixture and leave it on the stove until the liquid evaporates. Then remove it and add the thyme.

Fill the calamari tubes with 4 - 5 teaspoons of the prepared filling very carefully. Close them with toothpicks. Heat a grill pan. Brush it with olive oil. Put the stuffed calamari to bake in the grill pan for 5 - 6 minutes as turning them several times. Serve them warm with vegetable salad.

Combines with:

Vegetable salads and vegetable soups - without potatoes; to them may be added fish, seafood, fish caviar, mushrooms, olives (prepared according to the recipes of this book).

55.1. FRESH POTATOES WITH VEGETABLES IN OVEN

Ingredients for 4 servings:
- 2 lbs. (907 g.) fresh potatoes
- 5 oz. (150 g.) okra
- 2 medium zucchini
- 7 oz. (200 g.) roma tomatoes
- 1 yellow onion
- 1-2 cloves finely chopped garlic
- 2-3 tablespoons vegetable oil

Spices: 2 teaspoons paprika, 1-2 tablespoons finely chopped parsley, 1-2 sprigs fresh oregano, salt to taste

Way of preparation:
Preheat the oven to 390 F / 200 C.

Peel and cut the onion into thin slices. Peel and cut into rings the potatoes, zucchini and tomatoes. Cut the stems of the okra. In a small baking tray arrange one layer potatoes, one layer zucchini, one layer okra with garlic and oregano, one layer tomatoes.

Sprinkle with paprika, salt and the onion. Pour the dish with the oil and 1 cup of hot water. Bake the dish for 40 minutes. Serve it warm, sprinkle it with parsley.

Combines with:

Vegetable salads and vegetable soups - without meat ; to them may be added potatoes, mushrooms, olives (prepared according to the recipes of this book).

56.1. PORK STEW WITH RED PEPPERS

Ingredients for 4 servings:
- 24 oz. (680 g.) Boneless Pork Stew Meat
- 2 red sweet peppers
- 2 yellow onions
- 1 small cucumber
- 4 oz. (113 g.) fresh field mushrooms
- ½ cup white wine
- 1 tablespoon tomato sauce
- 3 tablespoons vegetable oil

Spices: ground black pepper and salt to taste.

Way of preparation:

Clean the mushrooms and cut them into quarters. Cut the cucumber in half along. Remove the seeds. Cut it in small pieces. Cut the peppers and onions into thin slices. In a pan heat the oil. Put the meat to stew on both sides for 5 - 6 minutes. Then remove it from the pan. Put in the pan the onions, peppers, mushrooms and tomato sauce. Stir the mixture well. When the vegetables soften, add black pepper and salt. Return the meat into the pan. Pour with the wine and continue stewing the dish. After 6 - 7 minutes, add ½ cup of warm water. Cook the dish until the meat softens. Add the cucumber and serve the dish warm.

Combines with:

Vegetable salads and vegetable soups - without potatoes; to them may be added meat, chicken, ham, mushrooms, olives (prepared according to the recipes of this book).

57.1. FILLET OF MACKEREL WITH VEGETABLES

Ingredients for 4 servings:

- 1 lb. 12 oz. (800 g.) Fish Fillet of Mackerel
- 12 oz. (340 g.) tomatoes
- 1-2 red sweet peppers
- 2 yellow onions
- 1-2 medium carrots
- ½ lemon – cut into rings (without skin)
- ½ cup white wine
- 1-2 tablespoons oil

Spices: 2 tablespoons finely chopped parsley, ground black pepper and salt to taste.

Way of preparation:

Cut the peppers into thin strips, onion - into slices, carrots and tomatoes – into rings.

Stew the peppers, carrots and onions in the oil. Add the wine, lemon rings, black pepper and salt. Once the mixture is well stewed, brush with oil a baking tray and pour the mixture in it. Cover it with tomatoes, pour them with ½ cup of hot water and arrange on top the fillets fish. Bake the dish 392 F / 200 C for about 20-30 minutes. Serve it warm, sprinkle it with parsley.

Combines with:

Vegetable salads and vegetable soups - without potatoes; to them may be added fish, seafood, fish caviar, mushrooms, olives (prepared according to the recipes of this book).

58.1. LASAGNA WITH ZUCCHINI AND BEEF

Ingredients for 4 servings:

- 2 lbs. (907 g.) zucchini
- 1 lb. (454 g.) Ground Beef
- 1 yellow onion
- 2 cloves garlic

- 3 large tomatoes
- 1 medium carrot
- 4 tablespoons vegetable oil

Spices: 1 tablespoon finely chopped dill and 2 tablespoons finely chopped parsley, a pinch of cumin, 1 teaspoon Worcestershire sauce, ground black pepper and salt to taste.

Way of preparation:

Preheat the oven to 392 F / 200 C. Cut the tomatoes and zucchini into rings.

Finely chop the carrot, onions and garlic. Stew them with 3 tablespoons of oil for 5-6 minutes. Add the minced meat, sprinkle with black pepper, cumin, 1 teaspoon Worcestershire sauce, salt and parsley. Grease a small deep tray with oil. Arrange one raw of tomatoes, over them place the half of the zucchini, then the meat mixture. Then again, one raw of zucchini, and then finish with tomatoes. Pour the dish with ½ cup of hot water and the remaining oil. Bake the dish in the oven for 40-50 minutes. Serve the dish warm, sprinkle it with dill.

Combines with:

Vegetable salads and vegetable soups - without potatoes; to them may be added meat, chicken, ham, mushrooms, olives (prepared according to the recipes of this book).

59.1. SALMON FILLET WITH ASPARAGUS

Ingredients for 4 servings:

- 1 lb. 5 oz. (600 g.) Salmon Fillet
- 12 oz. (340 g.) fresh asparagus
- 1-2 cloves garlic

Spices: ground black pepper and salt to taste.

For the sauce: ½ cup white wine, 1 cup onion - cut very finely, 1 teaspoon butter, ground black pepper.

Way of preparation:

For the sauce: Stew the onion in butter. Add ground black pepper and white wine. Cook for 2 - 3 minutes.

Put the asparagus in a pan. Pour ½ cup of water, add salt. Sprinkle the fish with black pepper and salt to taste. Put it on the asparagus. Place a lid on the pan. Cook for 8 minutes. Serve the meal warm, then pour it with a little sauce.

Combines with:

Vegetable salads and vegetable soups - without potatoes; to them may be added fish, seafood, fish caviar, mushrooms, olives (prepared according to the recipes of this book).

60.1. FISH SEAFOOD WITH FISH IN OVEN

Ingredients for 4 servings:
- 20 fresh mussels with shells
- 1 monkfish (without head) or other sea fish
- 1 - 2 calamari (cut into thin rings)
- 12 raw shrimps
- 1 cup fish broth
- 2 roma tomatoes
- 2 yellow onions
- 2 cloves garlic
- 1 tablespoon minced almonds
- 3 tablespoons olive oil
- 1 tablespoon cognac

Spices: 1 bay leaves, 1 teaspoon paprika, ½ teaspoon chili powder, 3 tablespoons finely chopped parsley, salt and ground black pepper to taste.

Way of preparation:

Thoroughly clean with cold water the mussels and monkfish. The monkfish cut into 4 pieces. Stew them in a pan with olive oil. Remove them and place them on a baking tray. In the same hot oil put the calamari and shrimps for 2 minutes. Remove them and place them in the tray too.

In a separate pan, stew the finely sliced onion and garlic for 2 minutes. Pour them with the cognac. (optionally flambé them) Add the peeled and coarsely chopped tomatoes, bay leaf, paprika, chili powder and fish broth. Stew the mixture on low heat for 5 minutes. Add the mussels. Leave the mixture to cook for another 4 - 5 minutes (If there are mussels that have not opened, remove them from the pan and discard). Add the almonds, salt and ground black pepper to taste.

Preheat the oven to 428 F / 220 C. Pour the seafood and fish with the prepared sauce. Put the dish in the oven for 5 - 10 minutes. Serve it warm, sprinkle it with parsley.

Combines with:

Vegetable salads and vegetable soups - without potatoes; to them may be added fish, seafood, fish caviar, mushrooms, olives (prepared according to the recipes of this book).

AUTUMN - LUNCH

1.1. PUMPKIN CREAM SOUP

Ingredients for 4 servings:
- 1 lb. (454 g.) boiled or roasted (peeled) pumpkin
- 2 medium potatoes
- 1 onion
- 2 cloves garlic
- 1 teaspoon grated ginger
- 5 oz. (150 g.) of fresh field mushrooms
- 1 teaspoon butter

Spices: juice from ½ lemon, ground black pepper and salt to taste, 1.5 oz. (40 g.) of raw peeled pumpkin seeds.

Way of preparation:

Peel the potatoes, cut them into small pieces and pour over them the water. Add salt and cook them until tender.

Finely chop the onion and garlic. Put in a pan the butter, the ginger, the onion and the garlic. Stir the mixture and then simmer for 2-3 minutes. Add the potatoes and pumpkin. After 2-3 minutes, blend the mixture. Put it into a pot. Sprinkle it with salt and pepper to taste. Add 4 cups of hot water. Allow the soup to boil 3-4 minutes and add the mushrooms. After 5-6 minutes, remove the pan from the heat and add the lemon juice.

Serve the soup hot. Sprinkle each serving with pumpkin seeds.

<u>Serve with:</u> *Pumpkin Stew*

1.2. PUMPKIN STEW

Ingredients for 4 servings:
- 26 oz. (737 g.) peeled raw pumpkin
- 14 oz. (400 g.) green zucchini
- 1 medium eggplant
- 1 medium onion
- 1 large carrot
- 1 red sweet pepper

- 2 ribs celery
- 2 tablespoons vegetable oil

Spices: 1 bay leaf, crushed dried chili pepper, a pinch of ground cumin, a pinch of grated nutmeg, ground pepper and salt to taste, 1 tablespoon finely chopped parsley.

Way of preparation:

Peel, clean and cut into large dice all the vegetables and the pumpkin. Heat the oil in a deep pan. Put the sliced vegetables to smother with a pinch of salt. Put the lid and after 6 minutes, add spices and 1-cup hot water. Preheat the oven to 392 F / 200 C. Transfer vegetable mixture in the pan and put it in the oven. Allow the dish to cook until the liquid evaporates. Serve sprinkled with parsley.

2.1. BEEF STEAK WITH PORCINI

Ingredients for 4 servings:

- 4 Beef Steak
- 5 oz. (142 g.) fresh porcini mushrooms (or 2 oz. dried porcini mushrooms)
- 1 teaspoon butter

For the marinade: ½ cup red wine, 1 tablespoon mustard, juice from ½ lemon, 1 teaspoon finely chopped chili pepper, 2 cloves crushed garlic, a pinch of ground black pepper.

Way of preparation:

Prepare the marinade. Put all ingredients in a bowl. Mix them vigorously. Place the steaks in the pan. Pour over them with marinade. Cover them with foil. Put the tray in the refrigerator for 4 hours. From time to time, turn round the stacks. Preheat the grill and bake them turning round in every in 7 minutes. Place the marinade in a pan and leave to simmer over medium heat until the sauce thickens.

Clean the mushrooms. Melt the butter in a pan. Cut the mushrooms into slices. Cook them for 5 minutes. Then sprinkle with ground black pepper and salt to taste. Serve them warm to hot roasted steaks. Pour over them with sauce, if desired.

<u>Combines with:</u>

Vegetable salads and vegetable soups - without potatoes; to them may be added meat, chicken, ham, mushrooms, olives (prepared according to the recipes of this book).

3.1. LASAGNA WITH BEEF

Ingredients for 4 servings:

- 1 lb. (454 g.) Ground Beef
- 1 onion
- 2 cloves garlic
- ½ cup celery, finely chopped
- 1 medium eggplants
- 2 green zucchini
- 7 roma tomatoes (could be used canned)
- 2 large tomatoes
- 2 tablespoons oil
- 1 teaspoon butter

Spices: 3 tablespoons finely chopped parsley, 1 teaspoon paprika, a pinch of grated nutmeg, ½ tablespoon rosemary, 1 teaspoon cumin, ground black pepper and salt to taste.

Way of preparation:

Finely chop the onion, the garlic and the celery. Wash eggplants and the zucchini, cut them into thin slices lengthwise. Peel 3 tomatoes and grate them coarsely. The remaining 3 tomatoes cut into circles. Salt the eggplants and let them stand for 20 minutes, then drain them well. Heat the oil in deep pan. Put the onion and the celery; stir them. After 3 minutes, add the meat and spices (except the parsley). Sauté the mixture for about 20 minutes. Grease deep tray or fireproof container with oil. Arrange the eggplants on the bottom sprinkle them with parsley and spread ½ of mixture of the minced meat. Arrange the eggplants on it; sprinkle with parsley, cover them with the remaining mixture of minced meat with spices. Pour over the dish with 1/3 cup hot water. On the top place close to each other circles of tomatoes. On each of them put the butter. Preheat the oven to 392 F / 200 C. Put the tray in the oven. Bake the dish for 40 - 50 minutes. Serve it warm, sprinkled with parsley.

Combines with:

Vegetable salads and vegetable soups - without potatoes; to them may be added meat, chicken, ham, mushrooms, olives (prepared according to the recipes of this book).

4.1. SOUP WITH LEEKS AND CELERY

Ingredients for 4 servings:

- 2 leeks
- 2 ribs celery or celery slices
- 7 oz. (200 g.) roma tomatoes (can be used canned)
- 2 cloves garlic
- ½ tablespoon tomato paste
- 2 tablespoons sunflower oil
- 4 cups chicken broth

Spices: 2 tablespoons finely chopped parsley, ground pepper and salt to taste.

Way of preparation:

Chop the leeks, celery and garlic. Sauté them in a pan with sunflower oil and 3-4 tablespoons of water. Sprinkle with pepper and salt to taste. Peel and chop the tomatoes into small pieces. Add them to tomato sauce in the pan. After 3-4 minutes, add the chicken broth. Simmer the soup about 15-20 minutes. Remove it from the fire. Sprinkle it with parsley. Serve the soup hot.

Serve with: *White Fish with Horseradish Sauce*

4.2 . WHITE FISH WITH HORSERADISH SAUCE

Ingredients for 4 servings:

- 28 oz. (800 g.) white fish, cleaned and without bones

- 1 ½ tablespoon olive oil
- ½ tablespoon finely grated horseradish root
- 1 teaspoon mustard
- 1 tablespoon chopped dill

For the broth: 1 liter of water, 2 tablespoons vinegar, 2 carrots-cut into rings, 1 stalk leek cut into pieces, 1 bay leaf, 4-5 sprigs of dill, 5-6 parsley, salt to taste.

Way of preparation:

Put in deep pot water and all products for the broth. Allow to boil for 30 minutes. Then add the fish. Cover with the lid and then cook on low heat 15-20 minutes. Remove the cooked fish and place it in large bowl. Strain the broth. Prepare the sauce: heat the olive oil, add horseradish, 4-5 tablespoons of the broth, mustard and dill. Mix and after 30 seconds, remove the pan. Pour over the fish with the prepared sauce and serve it.

5.1. CHICKEN WITH MUSHROOM SAUCE

Ingredients for 4 servings:

- 25 oz. (708 g.) Chicken Quarters
- 7 oz. (200 g.) of fresh aromatic mushrooms
- 1 medium carrot
- 1-2 ribs celery
- 1 medium onion
- 1 teaspoon butter
- 1 clove garlic
- ½ cup white wine

Spices: 15 black peppercorns, 1 tablespoon finely chopped oregano, ground black pepper and salt to taste.

Way of preparation:

Peel and cut into large pieces the carrot, the onion and the celery. Cut the chicken into portions. Put them in a deep saucepan. Pour over them with 3 cups of cold water. Leave to cook on medium heat. Once the water starts to boil, take the foam. Add the vegetables, black pepper and salt to taste. When the meat is cooked, strain the broth. Take the chicken pieces.

Then prepare the mushroom sauce. Cut the mushrooms into small pieces. Heat a pan and put the butter to melt. Add the garlic and the mushrooms, sprinkle with pepper. Cook them for 5 minutes. Add the wine and 1 cup of chicken broth. Cook them over high heat. After 8 minutes, remove the pan from the fire. Serve warm. In each plate put 1 portion chicken. Pour over it with 1 - 2 tablespoons of mushroom sauce. Sprinkle the dish with chopped oregano.

Serve with: *Salad of Beetroot and Carrots*

5.2. SALAD OF BEETROOT AND CARROTS

Ingredients for 4 servings:
- 1 medium head beetroot
- 2 medium carrots
- teaspoon grated fresh ginger
- 1 clove pressed garlic
- tablespoons sunflower seeds

Spices: 2 tablespoons vegetable oil (olive oil), 2 tablespoons lemon juice, 2 tablespoons finely chopped parsley, salt to taste.

Way of preparation:

Peel, wash and grate coarsely the red beets and the carrots. Put them in a deep bowl. Add ginger and garlic. Mix the salad well. Sprinkle it with olive oil, lemon juice, parsley. Sprinkle it with sunflower seeds and serve.

6.1. MEATBALLS IN TOMATO SAUCE

Ingredients for 4 servings:
- 7 oz. (200 g.) Ground Beef
- 14 oz. (400 g.) Ground Pork Meat
- 1 onion
- 8 roma tomatoes (could be used canned)
- ½ tablespoon tomato paste

- 2-3 cloves garlic
- 3 tablespoons oil

Spices: 1 teaspoon red pepper, 3 tablespoons finely chopped parsley, 10 fresh basil leaves (or parsley), ground black pepper and salt to taste.

Way of preparation:

Mix the minced meat, 2 tablespoons parsley, salt and ground black pepper to taste. After all products are mixed, add 2-3 tablespoons of cold water and continue to knead. Brush your hands with oil. Shape into 20 small balls of equal size. Cut the onion very finely. Heat oil and sauté the onion for 3-4 minutes. Then add the garlic, paprika, tomato paste, salt and the chopped tomatoes. After a few minutes, add 1 cup of hot water. When the mixture boils, drop in it the meatballs one by one. Cook the dish on low heat 40 minutes. Sprinkle the finished dish with parsley. Serve it warm. Garnish each serving with a few basil leaves (parsley).

Serve with: Black Turnip Salad

6.2. BLACK TURNIP SALAD

Ingredients for 4 servings:

- 21 oz. (600 g.) black turnip
- 10 black or green olives pitted

Spices: 2 tablespoons finely chopped parsley, 2-3 teaspoons of sunflower oil, 1 tablespoon wine vinegar, 2 cloves crushed garlic, salt to taste.

Way of preparation:

Peel and grate the turnip coarsely on a grater. Cut the olives into quarters. At the bottom of a deep bowl, mix oil, vinegar, garlic and salt to taste. Add turnips and olives. Mix the salad well. Sprinkle it with parsley and serve.

7.1. BEEF STEW WITH FRESH HERBS

Ingredients for 4 servings:

- 2 lb. 9 oz. (708 g.) Beef Rump Roast
- 2 oz. (57 g.) bacon
- 1 small head of garlic
- 1 onion
- ½ cup white wine
- 2 tablespoons oil
- 1 teaspoon butter

Spices: 2 sprigs of thyme and 1 rosemary sprig, 1 bay leaf, 2 tablespoons finely chopped parsley, 6 peppercorns, salt to taste.

Way of preparation:

This dish is cooked in a pressure cooker. Wash meat and flavor it by making small cuts and placing inside of them pieces of bacon, garlic and peppercorns. Put the whole piece of meat in the grill pan. Bake it for 2 minutes on each side. Then move it in a saucepan. Pour over it with 2 cups of water, wine and oil. Add the remaining spices and garlic cloves. Cover the pan and put it on low heat. When the cooker starts to emit steam from the valve, it is the time from which starts the cooking of the meat. There are necessary about 1.5 hours to cook the meat. Leave the meat in the pan until cool down. Then remove and let it cool. Cut it into slices. Cut the onion very finely. Put it to stew with ½ of the butter. Strain the broth from cooking of the meat and add 1 cup of it to the onion. When the sauce thickens, add the remaining butter and remove the sauce from heat. Serve the meat cold, pour over it with hot sauce.

Combines with:

Vegetable salads and vegetable soups - without potatoes; to them may be added meat, chicken, ham (prepared according to the recipes of this book), mustard, mushrooms, olives.

8.1. STUFFED BELL PEPPERS WITH PORK MEAT

Ingredients for 4 servings:

- 4 large or 8 medium red bell peppers

- 1 lb. (454 g.) pork shoulder
- 1 small onion
- 2 roma tomatoes
- 2 tablespoons vegetable oil

Spices: 1 teaspoon paprika 2 tablespoons finely chopped parsley, salt and ground black pepper to taste, a pinch of chilli (optional).

Way of preparation:

Cut the caps together with the stems of peppers. Clean the seeds and wash them. Chop the meat with a sharp knife of many tiny pieces. Cut 1 tomato very finely, and the other one on 4 (8) circles. Peel the onion and chop it very finely. Heat a pan and put 1 tablespoon oil to warm. Put onions to stew for 3 minutes. Add the meat, stir and add the paprika and chilli (optional). Leave to sauté over low heat about 10 minutes. Then add the chopped tomato, pepper and salt. Allow the mixture on the fire until the liquid evaporates. Then remove and allow to cool. Add parsley and fill the peppers with the mixture. Place one circle tomato and flaps to close the hole in the pod. Then arrange them in a tray. Pour over them with ½ cup of water and the remaining oil. Preheat oven to 392 F / 200 C. Roast on low heat for 30 minutes. Serve by one (or 2) stuffed pepper for each portion. Pour over it with 1 tablespoon of sauce left in the pan after baking.

Combines with:

Vegetable salads and vegetable soups - without potatoes; to them may be added meat, chicken, ham (prepared according to the recipes of this book), mushrooms, olives.

9.1. SOUP OF CHICKEN MEATBALLS

Ingredients for 4 servings:

- 9 oz. (255 g.) minced chicken (skinless breast)
- 2 leeks
- 4 oz. (113 g.) fresh mushrooms
- 2 red sweet peppers
- 2 ribs celery

- 1 teaspoon butter

Spices: 1 clove crushed garlic, a pinch of ginger powder, ground black pepper and salt to taste, the juice of 1 lemon.

Way of preparation:

Knead the minced chicken, ginger, garlic, ground pepper and salt to taste. From the mixture shape balls - with the size of a hazelnut. Chop finely and sauté the leeks, peppers, celery and mushrooms in butter. Once they soften, salt them and pour over them with 4 cups of warm water. When the water boils drop the balls one by one. Cook the soup for 30 minutes. Serve it warm. Optionally you can season it with ground pepper and lemon juice.

Serve with: Cauliflower Gratin

9.2. CAULIFLOWER GRATIN

Ingredients for 4 servings:

- 1 small head fresh cauliflower
- 1 large carrot
- 1 small onion
- 1 - 2 ribs celery
- 2 cloves garlic
- 3 roma tomatoes
- 3 tablespoons vegetable oil

Spices: 1 bay leaf, 2 tablespoons finely chopped parsley, 6 lemon slices, 6 peppercorns, and salt to taste.

Way of preparation:

Finely chop the carrots, onion, celery and garlic. Drop them in 2 cups of boiling water with salt. Add bay leaf and peppercorns. Cook vegetables 7 minutes. Then strain the broth. Take the vegetables on a baking tray. Clean cauliflower and tore it into florets. Put it in a saucepan with water and salt. Cook it for 5 minutes. Drain it and put it in the tray. Add tomatoes and parsley; stir the mixture. Pour it with oil. Place the lemon slices on top. Preheat oven to 428 F / 220 C. Put the pan with dish. Bake it for 30 minutes. Leave it in the oven to cool and serve.

10.1. PORK CHOPS WITH LEEKS

Ingredients for 4 servings:
- 4 - 8 Center Cut Pork Chops
- 2 leeks (white part)
- 1 large onion
- 5 oz. (142 g.) fresh champignons, chanterelles or other types of mushrooms
- ½ cup white wine
- 2 tablespoons vegetable oil
- ½ cup beef or vegetable broth

Spices: a pinch of ground cumin, a pinch of nutmeg, ground black pepper and salt to taste.

Way of preparation:

Sprinkle the chops with salt and pepper. In the pan heat 1 tablespoon oil. Put the chops, turn round them after 5 minutes. After another 5-6 minutes transfer them into a fireproof container (or baking pan). Cut the leeks and the onion into thin slices. Clean the mushrooms and cut them into chunks. In a separate bowl, mix the chopped vegetables, the mushrooms and the spices. Stir the mixture. Distribute it on the chops. Add the wine, the broth and the remaining oil. Put the lid (or the foil). Preheat the oven to 374 F / 190 C. Put in the oven. Allow the dish to be baked for 60 minutes. Turn off the oven and allow standing for 15 minutes. Then serve the chops. To each portion, add some of the vegetables and the mushrooms. Pour over them with 1 tablespoon sauce from baking.

Combines with:

Vegetable salads and vegetable soups - without potatoes; to them may be added meat, chicken, ham (prepared according to the recipes of this book), mushrooms, olives.

11.1. LEEK SOUP WITH POTATOES

Ingredients for 4 servings:
- ✓ 3 leeks
- • 2 ribs celery
- • 2 medium carrots
- • 2 Russet potatoes
- • 2 tablespoons vegetable oil

Spices: 3 sprigs of thyme, 1 tablespoon finely chopped parsley, ground black pepper and salt to taste.

Way of preparation:
Wash and slice the leeks and the celery very finely. Peel, wash and slice the potatoes and carrots into small cubes. Heat the oil in a saucepan on low heat. Add leeks, the celery, the carrots and potatoes to cook about 5 minutes. Stir the mixture well. Add the thyme, salt and pepper. Pour over the mixture with 5 cups of warm water. Simmer the soup over medium heat for 25 minutes. Sprinkle it with parsley and serve it warm.

<u>**Serve with:**</u> *Vegetable Stew*

11.2. VEGETABLE STEW

Ingredients for 4 servings:
- • 1 medium zucchini
- • 1 small eggplant
- • 1 red bell pepper
- • 1 cup green beans
- • 1 cup okra
- • 1 large carrot
- • 1 large onion
- • 3 Russet potatoes
- • 3 tablespoons vegetable oil

Spices: 1 tablespoon paprika, 1 teaspoon thyme (or savory), 3 tablespoons finely chopped parsley, salt to taste.

Way of preparation:
Peel the potatoes, eggplant, zucchini, onion and carrot. Cut them

into chunks. Wash the green beans and trim the ends. Clear peppers from the seeds and cut them into pieces. Wash the okra. Put all the vegetables in a deep pan. Sprinkle the mixture with pepper and salt. Stir it gently and add the thyme (savory). Sprinkle vegetables with oil and pour ½ cup hot water. Cover the pan with aluminum foil.

Preheat oven to 428 F / 220 C. Put the dish and bake 25 minutes. Remove the foil and leave the dish to bake another 20 minutes. Sprinkle with parsley and serve.

12.1. SPICY CHICKEN STUFFED WITH PORK

Ingredients for 6 servings:
- 1 small whole chicken
- 7 oz. (200 g.) ground pork meat
- 1 red sweet pepper
- 1 small onion
- 2 roma tomatoes
- 1 teaspoon butter

Spices: juice from ½ lemon, 1 tablespoon finely chopped parsley, a pinch of rosemary, 1 teaspoon paprika, ground black pepper and salt to taste.

Way of preparation:
Clean the chicken, wash it and dry it with paper towels. Smear it with lemon juice inside and out. On the inside sprinkle with pepper, paprika and salt. Prepare the filling. Finely chop the pepper, onions and tomatoes. Mix them in a bowl. Add the minced meat, rosemary and parsley. Stir the mixture well. Fill the chicken with stuffing and sew it up with thick thread. Brush the chicken on all sides with butter. Wrap it in aluminum foil and put it in the tray. Add ½ cup water into the tray. Preheat the oven to 392 F / 200 C. Put the tray in the oven and bake the chicken for 1 hour. Then remove the foil. Increase the heat to 428 F / 220 C and bake the chicken for another 10 minutes.

Serve with: *Vegetable Sticks with Appetizing Sauce*

12.2. VEGETABLE STICKS WITH APPETIZING SAUCE

Ingredients for 4 servings:
- 3 red sweet peppers
- 2 green sweet peppers
- 4 medium carrots
- 3 small cucumber
- 2 small zucchini

For appetizing sauce: 5 tablespoons olive oil, 1 ½ tablespoons vinegar, 1 tablespoon finely chopped dill, 1 clove chopped garlic, 1 onion chopped very finely, a pinch of ground black pepper, 4 anchovy fillets.

Way of preparation:
Wash, peel and chop all the vegetables lengthwise into strips. Put them in several high glass cups. Prepare the sauce. Mash the anchovy fillets and add the remaining ingredients. Mix them well. Put the sauce in a low glass bowl. Eat crunchy sticks dipped them in appetizing sauce.
The vegetable sticks are suitable for a party.

13.1. ROLL FROM MINCED MEAT

Ingredients for 4 servings:
- 1 lb. (454 g.) minced pork meat
- 8 oz. (227 g.) minced beef
- ½ cup white wine
- 1 tablespoon vegetable oil

For the filling: 1 teaspoon mustard, 2 small carrots - cut into small cubes, 2 onion - sliced, 6 oz. (170 g.) fresh mushrooms - cut into thin slices, 2 teaspoons butter, 2 tablespoons chopped parsley.

Spices: ½ teaspoon thyme, a pinch of coriander powder, a pinch of grated nutmeg, ground black pepper and salt to taste.

Way of preparation:

Mix the both types of minced meat, spices and 2 tablespoons cold water. Let the mixture stand for 30 minutes in the refrigerator.

For the filling: Heat the butter, add the chopped mushrooms. After 3 minutes, add the onions and the carrots. Sprinkle with salt and pepper. Sauté the mixture for 5 minutes. Then remove the pan from the heat.

Smear plenty a rectangular piece of parchment paper with oil. Spread on it the minced meat. Shape it into the shape of a rectangle. Smear it with mustard and place on it a part of the mushroom mixture. Wrap the roll by gently lifting the paper. Then remove the paper and place the roll in an appropriate oblong tray. Around it, distribute the rest of the mushroom mixture. Pour over the roll with wine. Preheat the oven to 392 F / 200 C. Put the roll and bake it for 40 minutes. Cut the finished roll into pieces with a thickness of about 0.8 inch (2 cm.). Serve the mushroom mixture as a garnish to each portion of roll. Sprinkle with parsley.

Combines with:

Vegetable salads and vegetable soups - without potatoes; to them may be added meat, chicken, ham (prepared according to the recipes of this book), mushrooms, olives.

14.1. SEA BASS WITH FENNEL

Ingredients for 4 servings:
- 2 whole fish (sea bass)
- ½ head fennel
- 6 green onions
- 1 yellow onion
- 2 red sweet peppers
- 2 ribs celery
- 1 large tomato
- ½ cup white wine
- 2 tablespoons vegetable oil

Spices: 1 tablespoon chopped parsley, ground white pepper and salt to taste.

Way of preparation:
Clean the fish and rub it with salt and white pepper inside and out. Cut finely the onion and the celery. Cut the fennel and the onion into thin slices. Clean the peppers from the stems and seeds; cut them into large pieces. Tomato cut into 4 circles. Heat oil in deep pan. Smother the fennel and the both types of onion for 6 minutes. Add the celery and the peppers. Sprinkle the mixture with salt and pepper. Cook the mixture for another 6 minutes. Remove the pan from the heat. To prepare this dish obtain oblong baking tray of fireproof glass. On the bottom put ½ of the vegetable mixture. Over it, carefully place the both whole fishes. Over them, add the rest of the vegetables. Pour over them with wine. On top, arrange tomato circles. Preheat the oven to 428 F / 220 C . Put in the oven (on lower level) for 30 minutes. For each portion, serve ½ fish and a few tablespoons of vegetables. Sprinkle with parsley.

Combines with:
Vegetable salads and vegetable soups - without potatoes; to them may be added fish, seafood, fish caviar, mushrooms, olives (prepared according to the recipes of this book).

15.1. AUTUMN SOUP WITH GROATS AND GINGER

Ingredients for 4 servings:
- 4 tablespoons groats
- 1 teaspoon grated ginger
- 1 medium carrot
- 1 root parsley
- 1 parsnip root
- 2 leeks
- 2 ribs celery
- 2 tablespoons vegetable oil

Spices: 2 tablespoons finely chopped parsley, ground black pepper and salt to taste.
Way of preparation:

Clean and wash the vegetables and the vegetables roots. Cut them into small pieces. Sauté them in a pan with sunflower oil and 3 tablespoons of water. Add salt and pepper. Add 4 cups of warm water. Cook the soup for 15 minutes. Then add the groats. Allow the soup to boil over moderate heat for 10 minutes. Then remove the soup, sprinkle it with parsley. Serve it warm.
Serve with: *Burgers from Groats and Zucchini*

15.2. BURGERS FROM GROATS AND ZUCCHINI

Ingredients for 4 servings:
- 1 cup groats
- 3 medium zucchini
- 3 green onions
- 4 tablespoons vegetable oil

Spices: 2 tablespoons finely chopped parsley, 1 teaspoon of curry, breadcrumbs for rolling the burgers, ground black pepper and salt to taste.

Way of preparation:
Cook the groats with a pinch of salt for 10 minutes. Then drain it very well. Allow it to cool. Grate the zucchini, sprinkle them with salt and let them stand about 30 minutes. Then drain them well.
In a deep bowl, place the groats, zucchini, finely chopped onion and spices. Stir the mixture well. Brush your hands with oil. Shape into burgers. Roll them in breadcrumbs. Arrange them in a baking dish greased with oil. Sprinkle the meatballs with remaining oil. Preheat the oven to   428 F / 200 C. Put the pan; cook the burgers for 20 minutes. Serve them warm.

16.1. LEEKS WITH EGGS

Ingredients for 4 servings:
- 8 leeks
- 8 eggs

- 4 tablespoons vegetable oil

Spices: 1 teaspoon of paprika, ½ teaspoon chopped red pepper, ground black pepper and salt to taste.

Way of preparation:

Peel and wash the leeks. Cut it into small pieces. Heat 3 tablespoons of oil, add the chopped red pepper and the leeks. Sauté them 6 minutes. Add salt, pepper and paprika. Stir and pour the mixture into the pan. Make 8 "nests" with the help of a spoon. In each one, break an egg. Sprinkle the eggs with salt, pepper and oil. Preheat the oven to 428 F / 220 C . Put the dish to be baked 15 minutes. Serve the dish warm.

Serve it with : *Stuffed Avocado*

16.2. STUFFED AVOCADO

Ingredients for 4 servings:

- 3 large avocados
- 1-2 roma tomatoes
- 1 small onion
- 2 cloves crushed garlic

Spices: 1 tablespoon olive oil, 1 small chili pepper, cleared of seeds and cut into very small pieces, juice of 1 lemon, 1 tablespoon finely chopped parsley, 2 sprigs fresh coriander, salt and ground black pepper.

Way of preparation:

Peel the tomatoes and remove the inner part. Allow to drain well. Then cut them into very small cubes. Cut two pieces of avocado lengthwise. Divide it in half and remove the pits. Using a spoon take the flesh of the third avocado. Mash it with a fork and pour over it immediately with lemon juice not to become black. Put it in a deep bowl. Add the finely chopped onion, the chopped tomato, garlic and chilli. Stir the mixture well, add lemon juice, parsley and salt, and pepper to taste. Fill the avocado halves with this mixture and leave it in the refrigerator to cool. Serve each portion in half stuffed avocado. If remain a stuffing, distribute it evenly in each portion. Garnish with coriander leaves. Sprinkle with a few drops of olive oil.

17.1. EGGPLANS STUFFED WITH CHICKEN DRUMSTICKS

Ingredients for 4 servings:
- 4 large eggplants
- 4 chicken drumsticks
- ½ tablespoon of butter
- 4 cloves crushed garlic
- 2 tablespoons vegetable oil

Spices: the juice from ½ lemon, 4 teaspoons tomato sauce, 1 teaspoon paprika, 4 grains allspice, ground black pepper and salt to taste.

Way of preparation:

Cut the cap with the handles of the eggplants. Carve them; sprinkle them with salt inside and out. Allow to stand 30 minutes. Then wash with cold water and dry with paper towels. Sprinkle the chicken drumsticks with pepper, paprika and a pinch of salt. Brush them with butter and bake them on a grill pan for 3 minutes on each side. Then remove and smear them with a mixture of lemon juice and tomato sauce. Rub the inside of eggplants with garlic. Put in each eggplant by one chicken drumstick. Arrange eggplant in the pan. Pour over them with a glass of water; sprinkle them with salt and oil. Put in a pan grains allspice. Preheat the oven to 392 F / 200 C. Put the tray in the oven. Bake the stuffed eggplants for 50 minutes. Serve them warm. Pour over each portion with 1 tablespoon of juice, which was removed during the baking.

Combines with:

Vegetable salads and vegetable soups - without potatoes; to them may be added meat, chicken, ham, mushrooms, olives (prepared according to the recipes of this book).

18.1. SKILLET BEEF WITH GREENS

Ingredients for 4 servings:
- 21 oz. (600 g.) Beef Stew Meat
- 3 green or red sweet peppers
- 6 roma tomatoes
- 1 large onion
- 4 tablespoons vegetable oil

Spices: 1 teaspoon paprika, 1 bay leaf, 2 tablespoons finely chopped parsley, salt to taste.

Way of preparation:
Heat the oil in a pan and put the meat. Stir it. Stew it for 15 minutes. Cut the peppers into strips, the onion finely. Add them to the meat. Sprinkle the mixture with salt and pepper to taste. Pour over it ½ cup warm water and add the bay leaf. Put the lid on the pan. Let the dish simmer on low heat 60 minutes. Cut the tomatoes finely. Add them and mix. Smother the meal about 10-15 minutes. Remove it from the heat and serve it after 10-15 minutes. Sprinkle each serving with parsley.

Combines with:
Vegetable salads and vegetable soups - without potatoes; to them may be added meat, chicken, ham, mushrooms, olives (prepared according to the recipes of this book).

19.1. PUMPKIN STUFFED IN RURAL

Ingredients for 4 servings:
- 1 small yellow pumpkin
- 1 sweet potato
- 2 red sweet peppers
- 1 yellow onion
- 2 cloves garlic
- 1 medium carrot
- 2 ribs celery
- 1 teaspoon ginger
- 1 parsnip root

- 4 tablespoons vegetable oil

Spices: 2-3 sprigs fresh thyme, salt and ground black pepper to taste.

Way of preparation:

Preheat the oven to 410 F / 210 C .

Wash the pumpkin. Cut a lid and carve it through a spoon. Discard the hollowed part and the seeds. Sprinkle the pumpkin from the inside with salt and pepper.

Peel the potatoes, carrots, onions, ginger, garlic and celery. Cut them into chunks. Peel the parsnip. Grate it coarsely. Take seeds from the peppers and cut them into chunks. Put all the vegetables and spices in a deep bowl. Stir the mixture and fill the pumpkin with it. Pour over with the oil. Put the lid of the pumpkin. Put it into a deep tray. Pour over it with 1 cup of water and put it in the oven to bake for 60-90 minutes. Serve warm.

Serve with: *Salad of Red Beets and Cucumber*

19.2. SALAD OF RED BEETS AND CUCUMBER

Ingredients for 4 servings:

- 21 oz. (600 g.) red beets
- 1 large cucumber
- 1 small onion
- 2 cloves crushed garlic

Spices: 3 tablespoons of sunflower oil, 1 tablespoon vinegar, salt and ground black pepper to taste.

Way of preparation:

Peel the beetroot and place it in a saucepan with water and salt to cook for 3 minutes. Allow it to cool and cut into thin rings. Cut the cucumber into thin rings and chop the onion finely. In a deep dish, arrange layers of cucumber and the beetroot. Salt each layer and sprinkle with oil and vinegar. Mix onion and garlic. Spread them on the top over the beet. Sprinkle the salad with pepper, salt and parsley and serve it.

20.1. BEEF SOUP WITH BEETROOT

Ingredients for 4 servings:

10 oz. (285 g.) Boneless Beef

- 1 small head of beetroot
- 1 medium carrot
- 1 onion
- 1 slice fresh cabbage
- 1 root parsley
- ½ teaspoon butter
- 1 tablespoon wine vinegar

Spices: 5 leaves of celery - finely chopped, 1 bay leaf, ground black pepper and salt to taste.

Way of preparation:

Peel the beetroot, onion, carrots and parsley root. Cut them into very small cubes. Cut the cabbage into very thin strips. Cut the meat into small pieces. Boil the meat gently in 2 cups of water, separate the foam from the surface. Add to the meat chopped vegetables, and 4 cups hot water. When meat is almost ready add beetroot. Sprinkle the soup with salt and pepper, add the bay leaf. Allow to cook until the meat is tender completely. Remove the soup from the heat, add butter and finely chopped celery leaves, stir. Serve the soup after few minutes.

Serve with: Foie Gras in Oven

20.2. FOIE GRAS IN OVEN

Ingredients for 4 servings:

- 14 oz. (400 g.) Foie Gras
- ½ cup red wine
- 2-3 tablespoons cognac

S*pices:* salt and ground black pepper to taste.

Way of preparation:

Sprinkle foie grass with salt and pepper. Put it in a small pan or bowl. Pour over it with wine and cognac. Let it stand in the refrigerator for 24 hours. Then put it in the pan, cover it tightly with aluminum foil. Preheat the oven to 374 F / 190 C. Put the tray into another deeper pan with hot water. In this way, the foie grass will be baked on water bath for 40 minutes. Serve it warm.

21.1. CREAM SOUP OF RED LENTILS

Ingredients for 4 servings:
- 1 cup red lentils
- 2 leeks
- 2 cloves garlic
- 2 tablespoons sunflower oil

Spices: 1 teaspoon paprika, 1 tablespoon finely chopped parsley, 2 sprigs of mint, salt to taste.

Way of preparation:
Wash the lentils thoroughly with cold water. Clean, wash and slice the leeks and the garlic into chunks. Heat the oil in a saucepan. Put garlic and leeks to cook 4 minutes. Add red pepper and pour 4 cups of water. Add the lentils and salt to taste. Cook the soup for 15 minutes on low heat. Then blend it. Sprinkle the soup with parsley, mint leaves and serve it warm.
Serve with: Chickpea Burgers

21.2. CHICKPEA BURGERS

Ingredients for 4 servings:
- 2 cups raw chickpeas
- 3 oz. (85 g.) fresh mushrooms
- 1 yellow onion
- 2 cloves garlic
- 2 tablespoons sunflower seeds
- 1 teaspoon of sesame
- 3 tablespoons olive oil

Spices: 1 teaspoon of cumin, a pinch of grated nutmeg, 1 tablespoon parsley, ground pepper and salt to taste.

Way of preparation:

Finely chop the onion and mushrooms. Heat 1 tablespoon olive oil in a skillet. Put the mushrooms and onions to smother until the liquid evaporates.

 Pour chickpeas with 6 cups lukewarm water. Put it in a pressure cooker. Turn on hot plate on heat at the lowest level. Leave the chickpeas to cook for 1 hour. Then let it cool and remove its skins. Put it in a blender. Add garlic, sunflower, spices, and stewed mushrooms with onions. Blend gently until smooth. Brush your hands with olive oil and form burgers. Sprinkle with olive oil and sesame. Preheat the grill pan. Put the burgers to bake for 7 minutes on each side, until golden brown.

(You can use canned chickpeas. In this case, thoroughly wash it with cold water).

22.1. SOUP OF TILAPIA AND MUSSELS

Ingredients for 4 servings:
- 10 oz. (285 g.) Tilapia Fillet
- 11 oz. (312 g.) Mussels with shells
- 1 small parsnip root
- 1 medium carrot
- 1 red sweet pepper
- 2 ribs celery
- ginger root (the walnut size)
- ¼ head fennel
- 2 roma tomatoes

Spices: 1 teaspoon ground coriander, 2 bay leaves, 2 twigs of fresh thyme, the juice from ½ lemon, 2 tablespoons finely chopped parsley, 4 slices of lemon, 10 peppercorns, salt to taste.

Way of preparation:
Clean the mussels. Wash them thoroughly with cold water. If there are open mussels, discard them. Peel the parsnips, carrots, celery and ginger. Cut the carrots into slices. Grate the ginger finely. Chop finely parsnips, celery and fennel. Clean the seeds from the pepper cut it in small pieces. Peel the tomatoes and cut

them into small pieces. Put in a deep pot 5 cups cold water. Add 1 teaspoon of salt and all vegetables (except tomatoes), pepper and coriander. Cook the soup and after 20 minutes, add the chopped fish, mussels, tomatoes, thyme, bay leaves and lemon slices. Cook the soup for 10 minutes. Remove it from the fire. Add lemon juice. Stir and serve the soup hot. Sprinkle each serving with parsley
Serve with: *Tomato Stuffed with Tuna and Basil*

22.2. TOMATO STUFFED WITH TUNA AND BASIL

Ingredients for 4 servings:
- 4 large salad tomatoes
- 1 can of tuna (85 g.)
- 1 small cucumber
- 1 red onion
- 1 lemon, sliced

Spices: 12 basil leaves, 2 cloves crushed garlic, the juice from ½ lemon, a pinch of ground black pepper, salt to taste.
Way of preparation:
Cut each tomato into two halves. Remove the inside of them. Let them drain on paper towels. Cut the onion. Wash the cucumber and cut it into small cubes. Break the fish into small pieces. Add to it the onion, the cucumber, garlic, 8 basil leaves, the lemon juice, pepper and salt to taste. Fill the tomatoes with this mixture. Arrange them on a plate and decorate with a slice of lemon and basil leaves. For each portion, serve two halves of the stuffed tomato.

23.1. SOUP OF BEEF AND CHICKEN

Ingredients for 4 servings:
- 7 oz. (200 g.) Short Beef Ribs
- 4 oz. (113 g.) Chicken Breasts
- 1 medium carrot
- 2 roma tomatoes

- 1 slice fresh cabbage

Spices: 1 bay leaf, 1 teaspoon cumin, 1 tablespoon finely chopped parsley, ground black pepper and salt to taste.

Way of preparation:

Cut the cabbage into very thin strips. Peel the carrot and tomatoes and cut them into small cubes. Boil the ribs well in 5 cups of water on low heat. Remove the beef ribs and remove the meat from the ribs. Cut it into small pieces and return to the pot. Then add the chicken cut into small pieces, carrots, cabbage, bay leaves, cumin, a pinch of salt and pepper to taste. Allow the soup to simmer for about 30 minutes.. Add tomatoes. Stir the soup and leave it for 5 minutes on the fire. Then remove and serve it warm. Sprinkle each serving with parsley.

Serve with: *Roasted Chicken Thighs with Carrots*

23.2. ROASTED CHICKEN THIGHS WITH CARROTS

Ingredients for 4 servings:
- 4 Chicken Thighs
- 3 large carrots
- 2 medium yellow onions
- 1 cup white wine
- 2 tablespoons olive oil

Spices: 1 teaspoon rosemary, ground black pepper and salt to taste

Way of preparation:

Sprinkle the chicken thighs with salt and pepper. Brush them with olive oil. Cut the carrots and the onions into thin slices. Put them in a deep pan. Sprinkle with pepper and rosemary; add the wine and ½ cup hot water. On carrots and onions, arrange the chicken thighs. Cover the pan with aluminum foil. Preheat oven to 392 F / 200 C. Put the dish and bake for 30-40 minutes. Remove the foil; pour over the chicken thighs with the sauce separated at the baking. Allow the dish in the oven for another 10 minutes. Serve the chicken thighs warm; pour over them with 1 tablespoon of sauce and add the carrots and onions for garnish.

24.1. VEGETABLE BROTH WITH CHICKEN DRUMSTICKS

Ingredients for 4 servings:
- 14 oz. (400 g.) Chicken Drumsticks
- 8 fresh small whole mushrooms
- 1 teaspoon butter

For the broth: 1 onion, 1 carrot, 1 parsnip root, ¼ small head of celery, 2 ribs celery.

Spices: 2 sprigs fresh thyme, 1 tablespoon finely chopped parsley, 1 bay leaf, a pinch of grated nutmeg, 10 peppercorns, a pinch of ground black pepper and salt to taste.

Way of preparation:
Clean the mushrooms. Heat the butter in a pan and add the mushrooms. Sprinkle with ground pepper and allow cooking for 7 minutes on medium heat. Then remove them and sprinkle them with salt to taste.

Peel, wash and chop very finely the onion, carrot, celery and parsnips. Clean and wash the chicken drumsticks. Put them in a large saucepan and pour over it with cold water just to cover. Once the water boils, take the foam. Add bay leaf, nutmeg, peppercorns, thyme and the chopped vegetables. Cook the soup over medium heat until the meat begins to separate from the bones. Then remove the chicken drumsticks, remove the skin and bones. Cut the meat into cubes. Strain the broth, put it in another saucepan and return it on the fire. When it boils up, add the mushrooms, the chopped meat and salt to taste. Cook the soup for another 10 minutes. Remove the pan from the heat. Sprinkle the soup with parsley. Serve it warm.

Serve with: Cabbage Stuffed with Meat

24.2. CABBAGE STUFFED WITH MEAT

Ingredients for 4 servings:

- 1 small whole fresh cabbage
- 7 oz. (200 g.) Boneless Pork
- 4 oz. (113 g.) Chicken Breasts
- 5 oz. (142g.) smoked bacon
- 1 small onion
- 2 cloves garlic
- 2 medium tomatoes
- 4 tablespoons vegetable oil

Spices: 2 teaspoons paprika, 1 tablespoon oregano, 2 tablespoons chopped parsley, ground black pepper and salt to taste.

Way of preparation:

Cut a lid of the cabbage. Carve it carefully. Put it into a pot filled with hot water and a pinch of salt. Leave it to cook for 10 minutes. Remove and drain. Let cabbage cool.

Cut the cabbage from below to stand steady.

Chop the pork finely. Peel and finely chop the onion. Chop finely the hollowed (the inside) part of the cabbage. In a deep frying pan heat 1 tablespoon oil. Put to sauté the pork, onion, garlic, ground pepper, red piper. After 10 minutes add the inside of the cabbage. Put the lid and stew on low heat about 15 minutes. Remove from the heat and add the oregano. Cut the chicken breasts and the bacon into small bites. Heat 2 tablespoons oil. Simmer about 10 minutes the chicken breasts and the bacon. Sprinkle them with pepper. Add parsley and stir. Fill the hollowed cabbage alternating stuffing of pork and the stuffing of chicken breasts and bacon. On top arrange sliced tomatoes circles. Put the cut cabbage lid. Pour over it with the remaining oil. Preheat the oven to 374 F / 190 C. Place the stuffed cabbage and bake for 1 – 1 ½ hours. Remove it from the oven and after 15 minutes serve it. Cut it as a cake.

25.1. RISOTTO WITH WHITE TURNIP

Ingredients for 4 servings:

- 1 ½ cup round grain rice (Arborio rice)
- 1 medium size turnip

- 1 cup of white wine
- 3 cups hot vegetable broth
- 1 sweet onion
- 3 tablespoons olive oil

Spices: 1 teaspoon oregano, a sprig of rosemary, ground black pepper and salt to taste.

Way of preparation:

Peel turnip and grate it finely. Wash it thoroughly with cold water and wring well. The rice for risotto should not be washed.

Heat 2 tablespoons olive oil in a saucepan with a thick bottom. Cut the onion finely. Put it in a pan and add the turnips. Cook them for 2 minutes. Then add the rice. Mix for 3 minutes, until the rice is transparent. Add the wine and continue stirring. When the wine is absorbed, start replenishing cup a cup of hot vegetable broth and stir. When you add the last cup of broth add all spices. Continue stirring until the liquid evaporates. Remove the dish from the heat, stir it and add the remaining olive oil. Serve it warm.

Combines with:

Vegetable salads and vegetable soups - without potatoes; to them may be added rice (prepared according to the recipes of this book), mushrooms, olives.

26.1. SOUP OF GREEN AND WHITE BEANS

Ingredients for 4 servings:

- 6 oz. (170 g.) green beans
- 2/3 cup white beans
- 1-2 leeks
- 1 medium carrot
- 1 small yellow onion
- 2 tablespoons sunflower oil
- 2 cloves garlic

Spices: 1 tablespoon chopped mint, salt to taste.

Way of preparation:

Clean the green beans, chop it into small pieces and wash it. Put it in a saucepan and pour over with 2-3 cups of cold water. Add salt. Put the pan on the fire for 15 minutes. In a separate saucepan, boil the white beans. Drain it and add it to the pan with the green beans. Heat the oil in a deep pan. Peel and finely chop the onions, leeks, garlic and carrot. Put them in the pan; add salt to taste. Stir the mixture and let it stew for 5 minutes. Then pour the mixture into the pan with the two types of beans. Add 2 cups of water and let the soup to cook for another 10 minutes. Remove the pan and add the mint. Serve the soup warm.

Serve with: *Peppers Stuffed with White Beans*

26.2. PEPPERS STUFFED WITH WHITE BEANS

Ingredients for 4 servings:
- 4 Red or Green Bell Peppers
- 1 ½ cups cooked white beans (may be used canned)
- 1 small onion
- 1 small carrot
- 3 tablespoons vegetable oil

Spices: salt to taste, 1 teaspoon paprika, 1 teaspoon ground red pepper (optional), 2 tablespoons chopped parsley, 1 tablespoon mint.

Way of preparation:

Cut the peppers caps on the handle side. Remove the seeds. Wash them with cold water and drain. In the pan, heat 2 tablespoons oil. Finely chop the onion and carrot. Smother for 10 minutes on low heat. Add salt, pepper and chili. Remove the pan from the heat and add the beans (if canned, wash it thoroughly with cold water and drain), salt, parsley, mint. Stir and allow the mixture to cool. Then fill the peppers. Put their covers. Put them in the pan; pour over them with the remaining oil. Pour ½ cup of warm water in the tray. Preheat the oven to 392 F / 200 C. Put the peppers to be baked about 30 - 40 minutes. Serve warm.

27.1. PORK AND CHICKEN WITH FRESH CABBAGE

Ingredients for 4 servings:
- 1 lb. (454 g.) Bone-In Pork Stew Meat
- 2 Chicken Drumsticks
- 25 oz. (708 g.) fresh cabbage
- 1 small onion
- 2 leeks
- 2 small carrots
- 3 roma tomatoes
- 4 tablespoons oil

Spices: 1 bay leaf, 2 cloves, 3 tablespoons finely chopped parsley, salt to taste.

Way of preparation:
Put in a deep pan the chicken drumsticks, pork meat and cold water, enough to cover them. Turn the heat. When it begins to boil, separate the foam. Cut the onion and leek on slices. Heat the oil and put them to suffocate with the bay leaf and the cloves. Stir the mixture and after 3 minutes add it to the meat. After 30 minutes, remove the chicken drumsticks. Take the meat from the bones. Shred the meat and return it to the pot. Clean, wash and chop the carrots, cabbage and tomatoes into thin strips. Add them in the pan with the pork meat. Put salt to taste. Cook the dish uncovered on low heat. Sprinkle the dish with pepper. After a few minutes, remove it from the heat. Serve the dish warm; sprinkle each serving with parsley.

Combines with:
Vegetable salads and vegetable soups - without potatoes; to them may be added meat, chicken, ham, mushrooms, olives (prepared according to the recipes of this book).

28.1. CREAM SOUP OF CAULIFLOWER

Ingredients for 4 servings:
- 1 fresh small head cauliflower
- 1 cup warm milk
- 3 ½ cups vegetable broth
- 1 teaspoon butter

Spices: zest and the juice of ½ lemon, a pinch of grated nutmeg 1 tablespoon finely chopped parsley, ground pepper and salt to taste.

Way of preparation:
Clean the cauliflower from leaves and cobs, tear it into small florets. Boil it in the vegetable broth. When the cauliflower is tender, take 4 roses and blend the others. Bring back the blended cauliflower in the hot broth. Add milk, lemon zest, pepper and nutmeg. After 5 minutes, remove the soup from the heat. Add butter and the lemon juice, sprinkle with parsley. Stir the soup well. Serve the soup hot into deep bowls. In each bowl put one of the torn florets of cauliflower.
Serve with: *Stuffed Brown Mushrooms with Garnish*

28.2. STUFFED BROWN MUSHROOMS WITH GARNISH

Ingredients for 4 servings:
- 2 lbs. (907 g.) large brown mushrooms
- 8 red bell peppers (for garnish)

Stuffing №1: 4 oz. (113 g.) Cheese "Cheddar" (can be used another kind of yellow cheese), ½ tablespoon butter, a pinch of ground black pepper.

Stuffing №2: 5 oz. (142 g.) Cottage Cheese, 1 tablespoon cream, 1 chili pepper, 1 tablespoon chopped dill, ½ tablespoon butter, a pinch of ground black pepper and salt to taste.

Way of preparation:
Bake the peppers on the grill, stove or in the oven. Put them in an envelope. After 30 minutes, peel them. Sprinkle with salt and serve them to the mushrooms for garnish.

Choose larger mushrooms. Clean them and remove their stumps. Prepare two types of fillings in two separate bowls by mixing the ingredients for each one separately. Fill one of the halves with mushroom stuffing and the other of the halves with the other stuffing. Arrange the stuffed mushrooms on a baking tray. Around them, arrange cleaned stumps. Salt them lightly. Preheat the oven to 392 F / 200 C. Put the tray in the oven. Bake the mushrooms for 15-20 minutes (until they are golden brown). Serve warm.

48.1. SPICY MEATBALLS WITH LEEKS OVEN

Ingredients for 4 servings:
- 13 oz. (370 g.) minced pork meat
- 9 oz. (255 g.) minced beef
- 1 small yellow onion
- 5 leeks (white part)
- 3 large carrots
- 4 tablespoons oil

Spices: 1 finely chopped chili pepper, 3 tablespoons finely chopped parsley, a pinch of ground coriander, a pinch of grated nutmeg, 2 sprigs fresh thyme, ground black pepper and salt to taste

Way of preparation:
Peel the carrots and the leeks. Cut them into thin slices. Cut the onion very finely. Put in deep bowl the minced meat, the onion, the chilli, the coriander, the nutmeg, the thyme, salt and pepper to taste. After mixing all products add a few tablespoons of cold water and continue to knead. Brush your hands with oil and form 8 equal-sized meatballs. Grease shallow baking pan with oil. Arrange the meatballs. Around them spread the leeks and the carrots, Salt them lightly and sprinkle with pepper. Sprinkle the meatballs and the vegetables with the remaining oil. Preheat the oven to 392 F / 200 C. Put the tray in the oven. After 10 minutes pour into the pan ½ cup warm water. When the meatballs get brown on the upper side, turn round them and continue baking.

Sprinkle the finished dish with parsley. Serve it warm.

Combines with:

Vegetable salads and vegetable soups - without potatoes; to them may be added meat, chicken, ham, mushrooms, olives (prepared according to the recipes of this book).

30.1. STUFFED CARP ON GRATIN

Ingredients for 4 servings:

- 1 Small Carp (about 3.5 lbs.- 1.500 g.)
- 3 sweet onions
- 3 roma tomatoes (could be used canned)
- 1 tablespoon tomato paste
- 1 lemon slices
- 3 tablespoons vegetable oil

Spices: 2 bay leaves, 3 sprigs fresh coriander, a pinch of grated nutmeg, salt to taste.

For the wine sauce: 1 cup white wine, 1 onion, 7 peppercorns, 1 bay leaf, 2 allspice berries, 2 grated tomatoes, 1 tablespoon oil.

Way of preparation:

Clean the fish from the viscera and scales in the direction from tail to head. Wash it with cold water. Dry it and rub with salt inside and out. Cut the onion into thin slices. Sauté it in oil for 3-4 minutes. Add the tomato paste, the finely chopped tomatoes and the spices. Leave to sauté until the liquid evaporates. Fill the carp with the stuffing. Sew the opening with strong thread (you can use toothpicks, also). If it remains part of the filling, put it into the pan in which you cook carp. Put the carp in the middle of the baking tray; around arrange lemon slices, pour over it with ½ cup water. Preheat the oven to 428 F / 220 C. Allow the dish to bake 20 minutes. During this time, heat the oil for topping and sauté in it the chopped onion. Add the wine, the grated tomatoes, peppercorns, bay leaf and allspice. Simmer the sauce for 10 minutes. Pour over the carp with this sauce and bake it another 10 minutes.

Combines with:

Vegetable salads and vegetable soups - without potatoes; to them may be added fish, seafood, fish caviar, mushrooms, olives (prepared according to the recipes of this book).

AUTUMN - DINNER

31.1. BEEF GOULASH

Ingredients for 4 servings:
- 22 oz. (624 g.) Beef Stew Meat
- 1 yellow onion
- 2 cloves garlic
- 3 red sweet peppers
- 2 ½ cups beef broth
- ½ cup white wine
- 2 tablespoons vegetable oil

Spices: 3 teaspoons paprika, 1 teaspoon cumin, ground black pepper and salt to taste, zest of 1 lemon.

Way of preparation:

Cut the onions, peppers and garlic very finely. Sprinkle the meat with pepper and paprika. In a deep pan heat the oil and put the meat. Stir it and after 5-6 minutes, add the onion, red bell peppers, garlic and cumin. Once the meat is browned, add the broth. Let the meat cook on low heat 90 minutes. At the end of cooking add the wine and salt to taste. After 10 minutes, remove the dish from the fire. Sprinkle it with lemon peel and serve warm.

Combines with:

Vegetable salads and vegetable soups - without potatoes; to them may be added meat, chicken, ham, mushrooms, olives (prepared according to the recipes of this book).

32.1. CHICKEN WITH BROCCOLI AND PINE NUTS

Ingredients for 4 servings:
- 1 lb. 6 oz. (624 g.) Chicken Breasts
- 21 oz. (600 g.) fresh cut broccoli crowns
- 1 medium carrot
- 1 teaspoon butter
- 1 cup hot chicken broth

- 1 tablespoon pine nuts

Spices: 2 tablespoons finely chopped parsley, 4 slices of lemon, ground black pepper and salt to taste.

Way of preparation:

Roast the pine nuts in a dry pan. Clean, wash and dry the chicken breasts. Cut them into pieces. Heat the butter in a deep pan. Put the chicken breasts. Sprinkle them with pepper and salt to taste, stir. After 6-7 minutes add, the carrots chopped into small cubes. Stir and after 3-4 minutes add the hot chicken broth. Wash and shred broccoli into small florets. Put them in the pan, sprinkle the dish with salt and ground black pepper, stir the dish. Let it cook for 10 minutes on low heat. Serve warm, sprinkle it with pine nuts and parsley. To each serving, add a slice of lemon.

Combines with:

Vegetable salads and vegetable soups - without potatoes; to them may be added meat, chicken, ham, mushrooms, olives (prepared according to the recipes of this book).

33.1. ONION CREAM SOUP

Ingredients for 4 servings:

- 4 large sweet onions
- 2 ribs celery
- ½ teaspoon butter
- ½ cup sour cream
- 3 oz. (85 g.) grated Cheddar Cheese

Spices: 3 sprigs fresh thyme, ground black pepper and salt to taste.

Way of preparation:

Cut the celery into small pieces. Peel and chop the onion into chunks. Melt the butter in a saucepan. Sauté the onion and the celery in butter for 10 minutes. Sprinkle with salt and pepper. Pour over them with 3 cups of hot water. Smother the soup over medium heat about 10 minutes, and then remove it from the fire. Blend it; add the cream and the thyme. Allow the soup to cook on

low heat for 3 minutes. Remove the soup from heat. Serve it warm. Sprinkle each portion with plenty of grated cheese.
Serve with: *Eggplants Stuffed with Mozzarella*

33.2. EGGPLANT STUFFED WITH MOZZARELLA

Ingredients for 4 servings:
- 2 large eggplant
- 10 oz. (285 g.) Mozzarella Cheese
- 1 tablespoon tomato paste
- 4 cloves garlic
- 3 roma tomatoes
- 4 tablespoons vegetable oil

Spices: 3 sprigs fresh basil (or 2 tablespoons finely chopped parsley), salt to taste.

Way of preparation:
Cut the eggplants in half lengthwise. Carve carefully with a spoon inside them. Sprinkle with salt and let it stand 30 minutes. Then wash them thoroughly with cold water. Put them in a deep pan with water to cook 10 minutes. Then drain them well. Apply them inside and out with oil. Brush just the inside of eggplants with tomato paste. On top add finely chopped garlic, basil (parsley) and cut into small pieces mozzarella cheese. Cut tomatoes into rings and arrange them on the mozzarella. Sprinkle with the remaining oil. Preheat oven to 392 F / 200 C. Put the stuffed eggplants to bake 30 minutes. Serve in each portion ½ eggplant.

34.1. SPICY BAKED MEATBALLS

Ingredients for 4 servings:
- 1 lb. (454 g.) Minced Pork Meat
- 9 oz. (255 g.) Minced Beef
- 1 yellow onion

- 1 ground red pepper
- 3 tablespoons sunflower oil

Spices: ½ teaspoon ground cumin, a pinch of grated nutmeg, 2 tablespoons finely chopped parsley, ground black pepper and salt to taste.

Way of preparation:

Chop very finely the onion and chilli. Combine all spices, the minced meat, onion and the chilli. Knead the minced meat, adding a little cold water. When the mince is sufficiently smooth, rub your hands with oil. Shape into 12 equal-sized meatballs. Preheat the oven to 392 F / 200 C. Grease a shallow baking pan with oil. Arrange the meatballs in it and pour over them with the remaining oil. Bake them for 15 minutes on both sides. Serve the meatballs warm.

Cooked in this recipe meatballs can bake and BBQ.

Serve with: *Salad Roasted Peppers and Tomatoes*

34.2. SALAD ROASTED PEPPERS AND TOMATOES

Ingredients for 4 servings:

- 12 red sweet peppers
- 2 salad tomatoes
- 4 roasted jalapeno peppers

Spices: 2 cloves finely chopped garlic, 2 tablespoons olive oil, 2 tablespoons chopped parsley, salt to taste.

Way of preparation:

Roast the red peppers on the grill, into the oven or on the stove. Put them for 15 minutes in an envelope. Then peel them and cut them into thin strips. Wash and cut tomatoes into small cubes. Arrange on a plate the sliced, roasted peppers. Salt them slightly and pour over with 1 tablespoon olive oil. Mix the tomatoes, garlic, a pinch of salt and 1 tablespoon olive oil. Stir them gently. Put them on the peppers. Sprinkle salad with parsley and serve it.

35.1. AUSTRALIAN PRAWN SOUP

Ingredients for 4 servings:
- 24 prawn
- 1 piece of ginger
- 1 yellow onion
- 1 red sweet pepper
- 2 roma tomatoes
- 3 cups fish broth
- 1 tablespoon fish sauce
- 1 cup coconut milk

Spices: a pinch of cayenne pepper, 3 sprigs finely chopped fresh cilantro, 2 tablespoons finely chopped parsley.

Way of preparation:

Peel the ginger and grate it coarsely. Peel and chop the onion and tomato into chunks. Clean the seeds of the red bell pepper and cut it into chunks. Put the ginger, onions, peppers and tomatoes in a deep bowl and blend them. Pour the mixture into a pan. Cook over medium heat about 4 minutes, stirring constantly.

Add the fish broth, fish sauce and red pepper. Stir again. Allow the mixture to boil, reduce the heat and cook 10 minutes. Add coconut milk and the shrimps. Cook over high heat, stirring constantly about 3 minutes. Reduce heat and cook another 3 minutes. Remove the pan from the heat. Add coriander and parsley. Stir and serve the soup warm.

Serve with: *Mussels with Lemon and White Wine*

35.2. MUSSELS WITH LEMON AND WHITE WINE

Ingredients for 4 servings:
- 3 lbs. (1.360 g.) mussels shells
- 3 leeks (white part)
- 2 cloves garlic
- Juice from ½ lemon
- 1 cup aromatic white wine

Spices: ground black pepper, a pinch of salt, 6 sprigs of fresh dill, lemon slices.

Way of preparation:

Clean the leeks. Cut it into chunks. Put it at the bottom of deep saucepan. Add garlic. Sprinkle with black pepper and a pinch of salt. Wash the mussels, clean them and put them in the pan. Discard the open mussels. Pour over the wine and lemon juice. Put the lid on the pan and leave mussels to cook over high heat. After 3 minutes, shake without removing the lid. After 3 minutes, shake again. After 4 minutes, remove the pot from the heat. Remove mussels (If there are mussels that have not opened, discard them). Garnish each serving with a sprig of dill and lemon slice. Serve immediately.

36.1. FRAGRANT CELERY SOUP WITH RICE

Ingredients for 4 servings:
- 5 ribs celery
- 1 sweet onion
- 4 tablespoons of rice
- 1 teaspoon butter

Spices: 2 tablespoon finely chopped parsley, ground black pepper and salt to taste.

Way of preparation:

Clean the onion and the celery. Cut them into small cubes. Put them in a saucepan. Pour over the vegetables with 4 cups of water. Add salt and pepper to taste. After 10 minutes, add the rice. When the ingredients become soft, remove the pan from the heat and add the butter. Serve the soup sprinkled with parsley.

Serve with: *Rice with Shallots in Oven*

36.2. RICE WITH SHALLOTS IN OVEN

Ingredients for 4 servings:
- 1 cup rice

- 1 lb. (454 g.) of small onions (shallots)
- 2 leeks (white part only)
- 2 cloves of garlic
- 12 pitted olives
- 1 teaspoon butter

Spices: 1 teaspoon paprika, 1 sprig mint, 2 tablespoons finely chopped parsley, ground black pepper and salt to taste.

Way of preparation:
Melt 1 teaspoon butter in a baking tray. Chop finely the leeks and the garlic. Put them in a tray. Preheat the oven to 428 F / 220 C. Put the tray in the oven. After 10 minutes, add the red pepper, rice, mint, ground pepper and salt to taste. Stir the dish, add 3 cups of water and let it bake. Heat the remaining butter in skillet. Sauté the small onions. When the rice in the oven begins to swell, add the stewed onions and the olives. Bake the dish until the rice absorbs all the water. Serve after 15 minutes. Sprinkle each serving with parsley.

37.1. BROCCOLI WITH FOUR CHEESES

Ingredients for 4 servings:
- 26 oz. (737 g.) Fresh Broccoli Crowns
- 4 oz. (113 g.) fresh champignons
- 3 oz. (85 g.) Cheese Gouda
- 3 oz. (85 g.) Cheddar Cheese
- 3 oz. (85 g.) Swiss Cheese
- 4 oz. (113 g.) Mozzarella Cheese for sprinkling
- 4-5 tablespoons sour cream
- 1 teaspoon butter

Spices: ground black pepper and salt to taste.

Way of preparation:
Cut the three kinds of cheese into thin slices. Grate Mozzarella cheese coarsely.
Take the broccoli florets. Put them in a saucepan with water and a pinch of salt. Cook them 7 minutes. Then drain them and place

them on a baking tray. Clean the mushrooms and cut them into chunks. Sprinkle with pepper and sauté them in butter for 10 minutes. Remove the container from the fire. Distribute the mushrooms over the broccoli florets. On them add three types of sliced cheese. On them put the sour cream and sprinkle with pepper.

Preheat oven to 392 F / 200 C. Put the dish and bake 10 minutes. Then open the oven and sprinkle the dish with grated Mozzarella cheese. Bake another 10 minutes, until golden color. Serve warm.

Combines with:

Vegetable salads and vegetable soups-without potatoes; to them may be added yogurt, cheese, cottage cheese, sour cream, mushrooms, olives(prepared according to the recipes of this book).

38.1. SOUP OF BEEF SHANK

Ingredients for 4 servings:

- 23 oz. (652 g.) Beef Shank Cross Cut
- 4 small onions (shallots)
- 4 baby carrots
- 2 ribs celery
- 1 parsnip root
- 1-2 parsley root
- 1-2 leeks (white part)
- 1 small tomato
- 2 cloves of garlic

Spices: 2 tarragon leaves, 2 tablespoons finely chopped parsley, salt to taste.

Way of preparation:

Pour over the meat with 7-8 teaspoons cold water. Cook them over low heat. Pick carefully collected on the surface foam. Shortly before the meat is tender, add salt to taste, the onions, the carrots (if they are bigger cut them into 2-4 pieces in length), parsley root and parsnips, leeks and celery cut into chunks, garlic cloves and finally the whole tomato. Do not add water. The meat and vegetables should be tender but not over boiled. Remove the soup from the heat and add the tarragon. Sprinkle it with parsley. Serve the soup hot. To each portion of the soup, put a part of all of the ingredients .

Combines with:
Vegetable salads and vegetable dishes - without potatoes; to them may be added meat, chicken, ham, mushrooms, olives (prepared according to the recipes of this book).

39.1. POTATO BURGERS WITH SEEDS

Ingredients for 4 servings:
- 27 oz. (765 g.) Russet Potatoes
- 1 sweet onion
- 2 cloves garlic
- 4 tablespoons vegetable oil
- 2 tablespoons raw sesame seeds
- 2 tablespoons raw sunflower seeds,

Spices: 2 tablespoons finely chopped mint (or oregano), 1 tablespoon finely chopped parsley, 1 teaspoon ground coriander, a pinch of nutmeg, ground black pepper and salt to taste.

Way of preparation:
Boil the potatoes for 20 minutes. Peel them and mash them well. Cut the onion very finely, blend the garlic. In a large bowl put the potatoes, onion, garlic, spices and 2 tablespoons oil. Stir the mixture carefully. Brush your hands with oil. From the mixture shape balls as big as an egg. Prepare a mixture of sesame and sunflower seeds. Roll the balls in this mixture. Arrange them in a baking dish greased with sunflower oil. Sprinkle the balls with sunflower oil. Preheat the oven to 410 F / 210 C. Put the tray in the oven. Bake the burgers about 20 minutes, until they get crispy crust. The cooked burgers are delicious both hot and cold. Serve with vegetables.

Serve with: *Cauliflower Salad*

39.2. CAULIFLOWER SALAD

Ingredients for 4 servings:
- 1 Small Head Cauliflower
- 3 red, yellow and orange mini peppers
- 8 olives

Spices: 2 tablespoons vinegar (or lemon juice), 2 tablespoons olive oil, 1 tablespoon finely chopped parsley, a pinch of grated nutmeg, salt and ground black pepper to taste.

Way of preparation:

Shred of cauliflower florets. Wash them and boil for 5 minutes in water with 1 teaspoon salt. Then drain them and immediately sprinkle them with vinegar not to darken. Sprinkle with nutmeg. Add cut into thin strips of mini sweet peppers and stir the mixture gently. Pour over with olive oil and place the salad in a serving plate. Sprinkle it with pepper and parsley. Garnish the salad with the olives.

40.1. PORK BONELESS SHOULDER ON LEEKS

Ingredients for 4 servings:
- 28 oz. (800 g.) Pork Boneless Shoulder
- 6 leeks (white part)
- 2 tablespoons vegetable oil
- 2 cups warm vegetable broth

Spices: 2 sprigs of thyme, 2 teaspoons paprika, 3 tablespoons finely chopped parsley, ground black pepper and salt to taste, 2 tablespoons mustard.

Way of preparation:

Wash the meat and dry with paper towels. Sprinkle it with black pepper and salt. Heat oil in a deep pan and add the meat (the whole piece). Turn it in order to brown on all sides. Add paprika, thyme and the broth. Put the lid on the pan. Let the dish simmer on low heat 70 minutes. Then remove the meat. Cut the leeks into thin rings. Put it in a deep saucepan. Sprinkle it with salt and pepper to taste. Put the meat on it. Strain the broth in which the meat was cooked. Pour over the dish with ½ cup of this broth. Leave to cook on low heat 20 minutes. Then remove the meat. Allow it to cool. Cut it into slices. Put the leeks in a large serving plate; sprinkle it with parsley. On it, arrange the sliced meat. Serve with mustard.

Combines with:

Vegetable salads and vegetable soups - without potatoes; to them may be added meat, chicken, poultry, mushrooms, olives, (prepared according to the recipes of this book).

41.1. CHICKEN CURRY AND CAULIFLOWER

Ingredients for 4 servings:
- 4 Boneless Chicken Breast
- 1 lb. (454 g.) Fresh Head Cauliflower
- 1 cup green beans
- 3 fresh roma tomatoes
- 2 cloves garlic
- 3 tablespoons sunflower oil
- 1 cup chicken broth

Spices: 1 teaspoon of curry, a pinch of ground cumin, 2 tablespoons finely chopped parsley, ground pepper and salt to taste.

Way of preparation:
Wash and dry the chicken breasts. Hammer them slightly and sprinkle with pepper and salt. Heat 1 tablespoon oil in a shallow pan. Put the chicken breasts, turn round them after 5 minutes. Let them bake the other side for 5 minutes. Wash the cauliflower florets, shred it and put it in a saucepan. Sprinkle it with salt and pour over with hot water. Cook it about 5 minutes, and then drain it. Clean and cut the green beans. Put it in a small saucepan with 2 cups water and a pinch of salt. Cook it for 15 minutes. Put in a deep pan the chicken, the cauliflower and the beans. Cut the

tomatoes, garlic finely, and add them. Sprinkle the dish with curry and cumin, stir it. Pour over it with broth and the remaining oil. Preheat oven to 392 F / 200 C. Put the tray, leave the dish and bake it for 30 minutes. Serve it warm. Sprinkle each serving with parsley.

Combines with:

Vegetable salads and vegetable soups - without potatoes; to them may be added poultry, meat, ham, mushrooms, olives, (prepared according to the recipes of this book).

42.1. TOMATOES STUFFED WITH EGGS

Ingredients for 4 servings:
- 4 large tomatoes or 8 medium tomatoes
- 8 large eggs
- 2 cloves pressed garlic
- 2 tablespoons vegetable oil

Spices: 1 teaspoon paprika, 12 basil leaves, ground black pepper and salt to taste.

Way of preparation:

Preheat the oven to 392 F / 200 C. Wash the tomatoes and carve them with a spoon. Sprinkle with black pepper and salt. Place in each tomato by a little garlic. Arrange them in an oiled tray. Break an egg into each tomato if they are of medium size (if tomatoes are large - break two eggs). Sprinkle with paprika and salt to taste. Put the tray in the oven. Bake tomatoes 10 minutes. Serve warm. Sprinkle each serving with a few basil leaves.

Combines with:

Vegetable salads, vegetable soups and vegetable dishes - without potatoes; to them may be added eggs, mushrooms, olives, omelets (prepared according to the recipes of this book).

43.1. CHOPS WITH TWO KINDS OF MUSHROOMS

Ingredients for 4 servings:

- 4 End Cut Pork Chops
- 4 large brown field mushrooms
- 2 oz. (57 g.) dried porcini mushrooms
- 1 large yellow onion
- ½ cup white wine
- 1 clove garlic
- 1 teaspoon butter

Spices: ground black pepper and salt to taste.

Way of preparation:

Finely cut the onion and the garlic. Clean the fresh mushrooms and cut them into strips. Soak the dried mushrooms in ½ cup cold water for 30 minutes. Then drain them and cut into strips (keep the water). Heat ½ teaspoon butter in a pan. Add the chops. After 5 minutes turn them round. After another 5 minutes, add the remaining butter. When it is melted, add the two types of mushrooms, the onion and the garlic over the chops. After 6 minutes, sprinkle the dish with pepper and salt; pour over with the wine and water, which was remained from the dried mushrooms. Put a lid, reduce the heat and cook the dish 30 minutes. Then remove from heat. Serve after 10 minutes with fresh salad.

Combines with:

Vegetable salads and vegetable soups - without potatoes; to them may be added ham, meat, poultry, mushrooms, olives, prepared according to the recipes of this book.

44.1. EGGPLANT ROLLS WITH GROUND BEEF

Ingredients for 4 servings:

- 14 oz. (400 g.) Ground Beef
- 3 - 4 large eggplants
- 1 large sweet onion
- 2 cloves garlic
- 20 oz. (567 g.) roma tomatoes
- 6 tablespoons vegetable oil

Spices: 2 teaspoons basil, 2 tablespoons finely chopped parsley, ground black pepper and salt to taste.

Way of preparation:

Cut the eggplant into thin slices lengthwise. Sprinkle them with salt. Allow to stand 30 minutes. Then wash them with cold water and dry them with paper towels. Sprinkle with oil and mix them. Preheat grill pan. Smear it with oil. Put the eggplants to roast. Turn round them after 5 minutes, and after another 5 minutes, remove them.

For the filling: Chop finely the onion and the garlic. Heat 2 tablespoons oil in a deep pan. Put the onion and the garlic; cook them for 3 minutes. Then add the ground beef. Stir and sprinkle with salt and pepper. Remove the pan from the heat. Add parsley and stir. On each eggplant put a little of the mixture of ground beef. Roll them; capture their ends with toothpicks. Arrange the finished rolls tightly in the pan. Grate the tomatoes, add the basil and pour over the rolls with this mixture. Preheat the oven to 392 F / 200 C. Put the dish and bake it 30 - 40 minutes. If necessary during the baking, pour a little hot water.

Combines with:

Vegetable salads and vegetable soups - without potatoes; to them may be added ham, meat, poultry, mushrooms, olives, prepared according to the recipes of this book.

45.1. STEW WITH SEAFOOD

Ingredients for 4 servings:

- 1 lb. (454 g.) fillets of sea fish
- 1 lb. (454 g.) mussels with shells
- 12 raw shrimps
- 1 sweet onion
- 2 cloves garlic
- 1 medium carrot
- 2 ribs celery
- 1 red bell pepper

- 1 lb. (454 g.) roma tomatoes
- 1 cup white wine
- 2 tablespoons olive oil

Spices: 3 sprigs of fresh basil (coriander), ground black pepper and salt to taste.

Way of preparation:

Clean the shrimps, leaving the tails. Cut the fish fillets into chunks. Clean the mussels, wash them thoroughly with cold water. Remove the opened mussels.

Cut the onion into slices. In deep saucepan put ½ of the onion, the garlic, 1 ½ tablespoons olive oil and the mussels. Turn on the heat and stir the mixture. Add the wine and put the lid on the pan. After 8 minutes, remove the pan from the heat. Take the mussels (If there mussels that have not opened - discard them). When cool, separate the shells. Strain the broth.

In a deep skillet, heat the remaining olive oil. Cut the carrot on rings. Cut the celery, the peppers and tomatoes into medium pieces. Put the vegetables (except tomatoes) in the pan. Add the remaining onion and the fish. Stew the mixture 7 minutes. Sprinkle it with pepper and salt. Then, add the shrimps and broth from mussels. Let the meat to cook on low heat for 5 minutes. Then add the tomatoes and mussels. After a few minutes, remove the pan from the heat. Sprinkle the dish with basil leaves (cilantro) and serve warm.

Combines with:

Vegetable salads and vegetable soups - without potatoes; to them may be added seafood, fish, olives, fish caviar, prepared according to the recipes of this book.

46.1. CELERY BURGERS WITH CRISPY CRUST

Ingredients for 4 servings:

- 1 Large Head Celery
- 1 lb. (454 g.) Russet Potatoes

- 1 sweet onion
- 4 tablespoons sunflower oil

Spices: 2 tablespoons finely chopped parsley, ground black pepper and salt to taste.

Way of preparation:

Boil the potatoes for 20 minutes. Peel them and mash them. Peel the celery. Cut it on chunks and put it in water with salt. Cook it about 20 minutes. Then drain and blend it. Cut the onion finely. In a large bowl place the celery, potatoes, onions, spices and 1 tablespoon oil. Stir the mixture carefully. Brush your hands with oil. Shape the mixture into croquettes as big as an egg. Arrange them in an oiled tray. Brush them with oil. Preheat oven to 392 F / 200 C. Put the tray in the oven. Bake the croquettes for 25 minutes, until they get crispy crust. So cooked croquettes are delicious both hot and cold. Serve them with fresh vegetables.

Serve with: Potatoes Roasted

46.2. POTATOES ROASTED

Ingredients for 4 servings:

- 24 oz. (680 g.) Russet Potatoes
- 5 oz. (142 g.) fresh champignons or any other type of mushrooms
- 1 sweet onion
- 2 teaspoons butter

Spices: 1 crushed red pepper (optional), 1 teaspoon butter to grease the baking tray, ground black pepper and salt to taste.

Way of preparation:

Wash and boil the potatoes in water with a pinch of salt for 15 minutes. Drain them and leave to cool. Cut them into thin slices. Cut the onion finely. Clean the mushrooms and cut them into chunks. Preheat in a skillet 1 teaspoon butter. Put the onion and mushrooms, sprinkle with pepper. Stew them for 10 minutes. Remove the pan from the heat and sprinkle the mushrooms with salt to taste. Prepare a baking tray. Brush it with butter. Put in baking tray a row of potatoes, mushrooms on them, on them second row potatoes. Spread the remaining butter on top. Preheat oven to 428 F / 220 C. Put the dish and bake 20 minutes. Serve it warm.

47.1. BEEF WITH ROASTED SWEET PEPPERS

Ingredients for 4 servings:
- 25 oz. (708 g.) Beef Stew Meat
- 3 red sweet peppers
- 2 cloves garlic
- 2 tablespoons vegetable oil
- ½ cup of wine

Spices: 1 teaspoon paprika, 7 peppercorns, 2 tablespoons finely chopped parsley, salt to taste.

Way of preparation:
Roast the peppers on the grill, stove or in the oven. Put them in an envelope. After 30 minutes, peel them. Clean the seeds and cut peppers into strips. Heat the oil and put the meat stew. Stir it once in a while. After 10 minutes, add the wine. After 10 minutes, add garlic, peppers, paprika, black pepper and salt to taste. Pour over it with ½ cup warm water. Put the lid on the pan. Cook the dish on low heat 40 minutes. Sprinkle the dish with parsley and serve warm.

Combines with:
Vegetable salads and vegetable soups - without potatoes; to them may be added ham, meat, poultry, mushrooms, olives, prepared according to the recipes of this book.

48.1. RED BEAN DUMPLINGS

Ingredients for 4 servings:
- 2 cups red beans
- ½ cup scallion, finely chopped
- 2 small pickled cucumbers
- 1 small carrot

- 2 garlic clove passaged
- 2 tablespoons vegetable oil

Spices: 1 tablespoon finely chopped mint, 1 tablespoon chopped parsley, ground black pepper and salt to taste,

Way of preparation:

Boil the red beans on low heat for 1.5 hours. (If you prefer, you can use canned beans. In this case, thoroughly wash it with cold water). Drain it and let it cool. In a separate pot, cook the carrot. Drain it and let them cool.

Cut very finely the pickled cucumber, scallion and the garlic.

Put in a bowl red beans and carrot. Blend them or mash them with a fork. Add to them garlic, scallion, pickled cucumber and spices. Stir the mixture. Brush your hands with oil. Shape into dumplings. Preheat a grill pan. Smear it with oil and place it on the stove switched to a medium level. When warm arrange the dumplings in the pan. Bake them for 6 minutes on each side. Serve warm.

Serve with: *Salad of Peppers with Eggplant Puree*

48.2. SALAD OF PEPPERS WITH EGGPLANT PUREE

Ingredients for 4 servings:

- 4 Yellow Bell Peppers
- 2 medium eggplants

Spices: 1 ½ tablespoons olive oil (or sunflower oil), ½ tablespoon wine vinegar, 2 cloves crushed garlic, 3 tablespoons finely chopped parsley, salt to taste, for decoration 4 olives.

Way of preparation:

Roast the red peppers and eggplants on the grill, in the oven or on the stove. Put them for 15 minutes in separate envelopes. Then peel them. Cut the stems of peppers and carefully separate the seeds. Peel the eggplants and remove the stalks. Mash them well. Add to them garlic, olive oil (sunflower oil), vinegar, 2 tablespoons parsley and a pinch of salt. With this mixture, fill the peppers. Arrange them on a plate. Sprinkle the salad with the remaining parsley. Decorate it with olives and serve it.

49.1. PORK RIBS BAKED ON GRILL

Ingredients for 4 servings:
- 4.3 lbs. (1.950 g.) Pork Loin Back Ribs

For the marinade: 2 tablespoons tomato paste, 2 tablespoons vegetable oil 3 cloves pressed garlic, ground black pepper to taste.

Way of preparation:

In a bowl, mix the ingredients for the marinade vigorously. Brush the ribs on all sides. Cover them with kitchen foil and leave them in the refrigerator for a 2 hours. Put the ribs to bake on the grill (or in the oven). Serve them warm with fresh vegetables.

Combines with:

Vegetable salads and vegetable soups - without potatoes; to them may be added ham, meat, poultry, mushrooms, olives, prepared according to the recipes of this book.

50.1. ROASTED CHICKEN STUFFED WITH GIBLETS

Ingredients for 4 servings:
- 1 small whole chicken
- 1 chicken giblets
- 3 large onions
- 6 roma tomatoes
- 1 teaspoon butter

Spices: 2 sprigs of thyme, ground black pepper and salt to taste 1-2 tablespoons finely chopped parsley.

Way of preparation:

Firstly, prepare the stuffing for chicken. Cut the chicken giblets into small pieces. Peel and finely chop 1 onion. Melt ½ teaespoon butter. Put the onion and the giblets. Cook them for 3 minutes. Remove the container from the fire. Sprinkle them with salt, pepper and thyme. Brush the chicken inside with butter and salt. Fill it with stuffing and sew it up. Sprinkle it with pepper and salt. Brush the chicken with remaining butter. Prepare a suitable baking pan. Pour into pan ½ cup hot water. Place the stuffed chicken in the tray. Preheat the oven to 392 F / 200 C. Bake the chicken 40 minutes. From time to time, pour over it with the sauce, which is separated during the baking.

Cut 2 onions into thin slices and finely chop the tomatoes. Put them around the chicken; sprinkle them lightly with salt and pepper. Allow the dish to bake another 10-15 minutes. Serve the roasted chicken warm, garnished with 1-2 tablespoons of onion and tomatoes. Sprinkle with parsley.

Combines with:

Vegetable salads and vegetable soups - without potatoes; to them may be added chicken, ham, meat, poultry, mushrooms, olives, prepared according to the recipes of this book.

51.1. RABBIT MEAT STEW

Ingredients for 4 servings:

- 1 lb. 12 oz. (800 g.) Rabbit Meat
- 2 tablespoon oil
- 1 yellow onion
- 3 cloves garlic

Spices: 6 salvia leaves, ground pepper and salt to taste.

For the marinade: 1 cup vinegar, 1 tablespoon oil, 1 small onion, 2 carrots, 2 bay leaves, 1 teaspoons thyme, 5 black peppercorns.

Way of preparation:

Cut the rabbit meat into portions. The marinade: mix the vinegar with oil and 1 cup cold water. Add the sliced carrots and the onion, bay leaf, thyme and peppercorns. Mix the marinade and put it on the fire to boil. Then let it cool. Pour over the rabbit meat with the marinade. Leave it in the refrigerator for 5 hours. Then remove the meat and dry it.

Heat the oil and sauté the meat for 7 minutes. Add the onion and garlic cut into thin slices, the pepper and salt to taste. Pour over them with 1 cup of the marinade. Put the dish to simmer on low heat. (until the meat is cooked). If necessary during the cooking add a little of the marinade. Remove the dish from the heat and add the salvia leaves. Mix and serve the dish warm.

Combines with:

Vegetable salads and vegetable soups - without potatoes; to them may be added chicken, ham, meat, poultry, mushrooms, olives, prepared according to the recipes of this book.

52.1. CRISPY CARROT CROQUETTES

Ingredients for 4 servings:
- 25 oz. (708 g.) fresh carrots
- 7 oz. (200 g.) head of celery
- ½ cup scallion, finely chopped
- 2 egg whites
- 4 tablespoons sunflower oil

Spices: 2 tablespoons finely chopped parsley, ground black pepper and salt to taste.

Way of preparation:

Wash, peel and cut coarsely the carrots and celery. Boil them in salted water for 15 minutes. Drain them of the water. Blend them well. In a large bowl beat the egg whites with salt. Add to them the smashed vegetables, the finely chopped scallion, pepper and parsley. Stir the mixture well. Preheat oven to 410 F / 210 C. Place an oiled pan to heat. Divide the mixture into 4 equal parts. When the oil is hot enough, remove the tray. With the help of a spoon, place the mixture in the four corners of the tray. Lightly press each part of the mixture to form large croquettes. Sprinkle them with oil. Put them to bake 20 minutes. Serve the croquettes warm

with salad.
Serve with: *Vegetable Salad with Mayonnaise*

52.2. VEGETABLE SALAD WITH MAYONNAISE

Ingredients for 4 servings:
- 1 slice fresh cabbage
- 1 slice head celery
- 2 medium carrots
- 1 yellow bell pepper
- 2 green onions
- 2 tablespoons finely chopped parsley

For the topping: 1 cup mayonnaise, 2 teaspoons mustard, juice of 1 lemon, ground black pepper and salt to taste.

Way of preparation:
Cut the cabbage into thin strips. Peel the celery and the carrots. Grate them coarsely. Clean the onion and chop it finely. Wash the peppers and remove the seeds. Cut it in thin strips. Put in a deep bowl all the chopped vegetables, stir them well. In a separate bowl, combine the ingredients for the topping. Pour over it with the vegetables. Put the salad to stand for 15 minutes in the refrigerator. Sprinkle it with parsley and serve it.

53.1. GROUND PORK MEAT WITH CAULIFLOWER GRATIN

Ingredients for 4 servings:
- ✓ 17 oz. (480 g.) Ground Pork Meat
- 1 medium fresh head cauliflower
- 1 medium onion
- 2 cloves garlic
- 3 roma tomatoes
- 2 tablespoons vegetable oil

Spices: 3 tablespoons finely chopped parsley, 2 sprigs fresh coriander, ½ teaspoon grated nutmeg, ground black pepper and salt to taste.

Way of preparation:
Divide the cauliflower into small florets. In a deep pan pour water and add a pinch of salt and cauliflower. Cook it for 8 minutes. Then drain. Finely chop the onion and cook 3 minutes. Add the garlic, the ground pork meat and spices. Stir and simmer the mixture for 5 minutes. Add cauliflower. Stir the mixture and pour it into a small pan. Cut the tomatoes into slices. Put them at the top tightly. Pour over the dish with two coffee cups warm water. Preheat the oven to 410 F / 210 C. Put the dish and bake 40 minutes. Serve it warm.

Combines with:
Vegetable salads and vegetable soups - without potatoes; to them may be added meat, poultry, mushrooms, olives, prepared according to the recipes of this book.

54.1. MACKEREL WITH TOMATO SAUCE

Ingredients for 4 servings:
- 1 lb. 12 oz. (800 g.) Mackerel Fillets
- 21 oz. (600 g.) roma tomatoes
- 3 cloves garlic
- 1 tablespoon vegetable oil

Spices: 2 bay leaves- crushed, zest of ½ lemon, 2 tablespoons finely chopped parsley, ground black pepper and salt to taste.

Way of preparation:
Arrange the fish fillets in a fireproof baking tray. Sprinkle them with pepper, salt and lemon zest. Sprinkle them with oil, add the garlic and chopped bay leaves. Pour over ½ cup water. Peel the tomatoes and grate them coarsely. Pour them over the fish. Put the lid of the baking tray or use an aluminum foil. Put the baking tray in cold oven. Preheat the oven to 428 F / 220 C. Allow the dish to cook 25 minutes. For each portion serve one fillet, on it put 2 tablespoons of tomato sauce. Sprinkle with parsley.

Combines with:
Vegetable salads and vegetable soups - without potatoes; to them

may be added seafood, fish, olives, fish caviar, prepared according to the recipes of this book.

55.1. BRUSSELS SPROUTS WITH MASHED POTATOES

Ingredients for 4 servings:
- 1 lb. (454 g.) Brussels Sprouts
- 22 oz. (624 g.) Russet Potatoes
- 1 yellow onion
- 2 teaspoons melted butter

Spices: 2 tablespoons finely chopped parsley, ground black pepper and salt to taste.

Way of preparation:
Clean and wash the Brussels sprouts. Put it in a large saucepan. Sprinkle it with salt to taste and add ½ cup water. Cook Brussels sprouts on low heat until the liquid evaporates.
Cut the onion very finely. Wash the potatoes and put them in a deep saucepan. Pour over with water; add a pinch of salt. Cook them for 25 minutes. Drain them and let them cool. Mash them well and add ground black pepper, salt to taste, 1 tablespoon butter and onion. Mix the Brussels sprouts and potatoes, stir them carefully. Serve hot in a large bowl. Make a well in the center and put the remaining melted butter. Sprinkle the dish with parsley.

Combines with:
Vegetable salads and vegetable soups - to them may be added potatoes, mushrooms, olives, prepared according to the recipes of this book.

56.1. TURKEY BREAST STEW WITH SHALLOTS

Ingredients for 4 servings:
- 22 oz. (624 g.) Turkey Breast
- 20 small shallots
- 4 oz. (113 g.) fresh chanterelle mushrooms or champignons

- 2 cloves garlic
- ½ cup white wine
- 1 cup chicken broth
- 1 teaspoon butter

Spices: 2 tablespoons finely chopped parsley, ground black pepper and salt to taste.

Way of preparation:

Cut the Turkey Breast into portions. Melt 1 teaspoon butter in a deep pan. Stew the meat 15 minutes. Add the wine, after 10 minutes, add 1 cup of broth (or warm water). In another pan, melt the remaining butter. Cut the mushrooms into large pieces and cook them with the shallots for 15 minutes. Sprinkle with salt and pepper to taste. When the meat is tender, add it to the mushrooms and shallots. After 10 minutes, remove the dish from the fire. Serve it warm; sprinkle it with parsley.

Combines with:

Vegetable salads and vegetable soups - without potatoes; to them may be added poultry, meat, mushrooms, olives, prepared according to the recipes of this book.

57.1. ONION STUFFED WITH BEEF AND BACON

Ingredients for 4 servings:

- 8 large sweet onions
- 6 oz. (170 g.) Ground Beef
- 4 oz. (113 g.) Smoked Bacon
- 5 oz. (142 g.) fresh mushrooms
- ½ teaspoon butter
- 3 tablespoons white wine

Spices: 1 tablespoon finely chopped thyme, 1 tablespoon parsley, a pinch of ground cumin, ground black pepper and salt to taste.

Way of preparation:

Cut the mushrooms into small pieces. Clean the onion and carve it. Finely chop the onion inside and stew it with together with the mushrooms in butter. After 5 minutes, add the minced meat and

the wine. Sprinkle the mixture with pepper, salt, parsley and thyme. Stir it. With this stuffing, fill the carved onions. On each onion, place 2 pieces of bacon. Wrap each onion on a sheet of aluminum foil. Put the sachets in the pan. Pour into the pan ½ cup warm water. Preheat the oven to 428 F / 220 C. Put the dish and bake it 40 minutes. For each portion, serve 2 heads stuffed onions.
Serve with: *Salad with Fresh Cabbage and Ham*

57.2. SALAD WITH FRESH CABBAGE AND HAM

Ingredients for 4 servings:
- 14 oz. (400 g.) fresh green cabbage
- 4 oz. (113 g.) cooked ham
- 2 medium carrots
- 1 medium cucumber
- 8 cherry tomatoes

Spices: 3 tablespoons finely chopped parsley, 2 teaspoons of sunflower oil, 1 tablespoons vinegar, salt to taste.

Way of preparation:
Cut the ham into very thin strips. Wash all the vegetables with cold water. Cut the cabbage into thin strips; the cucumber into thin slices; tomatoes into small cubes. Peel the carrots, grate them finely on a greater.
Sprinkle the cabbage with salt and mash with hands to soften slightly. Arrange vegetables and ham. Sprinkle with sauce made from oil, vinegar and salt to taste. Serve the salad after 5 minutes. Sprinkle it with parsley.

58.1. GOURMET STUFFED BEEF ROAST

Ingredients for 4 servings:
- 25 oz. (708 g.) Beef Rump Roast
- 8 pitted olives, cut into halves
- 2 small pickled cucumbers
- 1 red sweet pepper

- ½ cup white wine
- 1 lb. (454 g.) roma tomatoes (you can canned)
- 1 teaspoon butter

Spices: ½ tablespoon mustard, 2 leaves tarragon, 2 tablespoons finely chopped parsley, ground black pepper and salt to taste.

Way of preparation:

Wash the tomatoes and cut them into very small pieces. Cut the cucumbers and peppers into quarters lengthwise. Make an incision along the length of the meat with a sharp knife. Then cut along the entire length, to obtain a flat piece in the shape of a rectangle. Smear it with mustard. Spread on it the half of the olives, tarragon, cucumbers and peppers. Wrap the meat on roll and fasten thread. Heat the butter in a deep pan. Put the meat; sprinkle it with salt and pepper. Turn it until evenly browned on all sides. Add wine, cover with a lid and bake the meat in the oven at 360 F / 180 C. If necessary, top up with a little water until the meat is cooked. Then remove and let it to cool. In a pan, add tomatoes, parsley and the remaining olives. Allow the sauce to simmer until thickened. Before removing it, add salt to taste. Serve the meat cut into slices. Pour over with tomato sauce.

Combines with:

Vegetable salads and vegetable soups - without potatoes; to them may be added meat, ham, poultry, mushrooms, olives, prepared according to the recipes of this book.

59.1. FRESH CABBAGE STUFFED WITH BROWN RICE

Ingredients for 4 servings:

- 1 small whole cabbage
- 1 cup brown rice
- 1 small onion
- 4 tablespoons vegetable oil

Spices: ½ teaspoon of citric acid (or 2 tablespoons lemon juice) 2 teaspoons paprika, 1 teaspoon of ground cumin, 2 tablespoons finely chopped parsley, ground black pepper and salt to taste.

Way of preparation:

Cut out the bottom of the cabbage, so that it becomes flat. Carve and remove the solid portion on about 1.2 inch (3 cm.) Put it into a deep saucepan. Pour over it with hot water. Add 2 teaspoons of salt and citric acid. Cook for 10 minutes. Allow to cool, then remove, and drain it. Put it into a deep refractory container in which to cook the dish.

Prepare the stuffing as follows. Firstly, finely chop the onion. Put it to stew with two tablespoons of oil for 3-4 minutes. Then add the cumin, 1 teaspoon of paprika, rice, pepper and salt to taste. Stir and add 2 cups of water. When the water evaporates, add another 2 cups of water. Rice should cook on low heat 30 minutes. Then remove and let cool. Add parsley and mix the stuffing.

Carefully open the first leaf (the outermost leaf) of the cabbage and place a tablespoon of filling. Screw into roll. Then fill the next sheet in the same way. When you cannot open more leaves of the cabbage carve and put the stuffing that was left. Sprinkle the stuffed cabbage with red pepper and then pour over it with the remaining oil. Cover the dish with aluminum foil. Preheat the oven to 392 F / 200 C. Place the stuffed cabbage to be baked 30 minutes. Then remove the foil and bake another 10 minutes. Serve the dish warm.

Combines with:

Vegetable salads and vegetable soups - without potatoes; to them may be added rice, olives, mushrooms, prepared according to the recipes of this book.

60.1. QUAILS BAKED

Ingredients for 4 servings:
- 8 Quails
- 5 oz. (142 g.) Smoked Bacon
- 1-2 teaspoons butter

Spices: ground black pepper and salt to taste.

Way of preparation:

Clean and wash well the quails. Salt them inside and out; sprinkle with black pepper; coat them with butter. Cut the pork breast into very thin strips. Wrap each quail with pork strip breasts. Put them in a buttered pan. Preheat the oven to 392 F / 200 C. Put the tray in the oven. Bake quails for 30 minutes. Serve them warm with fresh vegetables.

Combines with:

Vegetable salads and vegetable soups - without potatoes; to them may be added meat, ham, poultry, mushrooms, olives, prepared according to the recipes of this book.

WINTER - LUNCH

1.1. PORK KNUCKLES WITH SAUERKRAUT

Ingredients for 4 servings:
- 2 lbs. 3 oz. (1.000 g.) Pork Knuckles
- 3 lbs. (1.360 g.) chopped sauerkraut
- 3 tablespoons vegetable oil

Spices: 1 teaspoon ground cumin, 3 teaspoons paprika, 1 teaspoon crushed red pepper.

Way of preparation:
To the chopped sauerkraut put the spices. Stir the mixture well. Cover the bottom of a deep saucepan with half of the amount of sauerkraut with spices. Put on it the whole knuckle. Cover with remaining cabbage. Pour over the dish with 1 ½ cups of warm water.

Put the pan on low heat. The dish should be cooked slowly, about 1.5 hours. Then pour in the pan. (If after cooking has remained liquid remove it). Remove the bone from the shank carefully, trying to keep it whole. Pour the entire dish with oil. Preheat the oven to 428 F / 220 C. Put the tray in the oven. Bake the dish for 15 minutes. Serve it warm in a large bowl. Put the whole knuckle in the middle of the plate.

Combines with:
Vegetable salads and vegetable soups - without potatoes; to them may be added meat, chicken, ham, mushrooms, olives, prepared according to the recipes of this book.

2.1. SOUP OF CHICKEN BREASTS WITH GINGER

Ingredients for 4 servings:
- 10 oz. (285 g.) Boneless Chicken Breast
- 1 small piece ginger root
- 4 oz. (113 g.) fresh mushrooms
- 1 sweet onion

- 1 medium carrot
- 2 tablespoons oil
- 4 cups chicken broth (or water)

Spices: 2 tablespoons lemon juice, 2 bay leaves, 1 tablespoon chopped parsley, ground black pepper and salt to taste.

Way of preparation:
Peel and wash the onions, ginger and carrot. Grate the ginger finely; chop the onion and carrot finely. Clean the mushrooms and cut them into small pieces. Heat the oil over medium heat in a suitable pot. Put the mushrooms and vegetables to smother a few minutes. Wash and cut the chicken breasts into small pieces. Add them in the pan. Sprinkle with salt and ground black pepper. Stir and pour the broth. After 30 minutes, remove the soup from the heat. Add the lemon juice and parsley. Serve the soup hot.
Serve with: *Chicken with Spicy Sauce*

2.2. CHICKEN WITH SPICY SAUCE

Ingredients for 4 servings:
- 24 oz. (680 g.) Chopped Chicken Meat
- 2 sweet onions
- 2 cloves garlic
- 1 teaspoon grated ginger root
- 2 tablespoons vegetable oil
- ½ cup white wine
- 1 cup chicken broth

Spices: ground black pepper and salt to taste, 2 tablespoons chopped parsley.

Way of preparation:
Cut the onions and the garlic finely. Heat a large pan. Place the oil to warm. Sprinkle the chicken meat with pepper and salt. Fry it for 4 minutes. Then, take it out on a plate. In the same pan put the ginger, the garlic and the onion. Stir the mixture until it is well smothered. After 3 minutes, add the wine and broth. When the mixture boils return the chicken meat in the pan (if necessary

add salt). Stew the meal on low heat until the meat is tender and the dish thickens (about 30 minutes). Sprinkle with parsley and serve the dish warm.

3.1. ROASTED CAULIFLOWER WITH GROUND PORK

Ingredients for 4 servings:
- 14 oz. (400 g.) Ground Pork
- 5 oz. (142 g.) Bacon
- 1 small head fresh cauliflower
- 1 onion
- 3 tablespoons oil
- 1 tablespoon tomato paste

Spices: 2 teaspoons Worcestershire sauce, 1 teaspoon grated nutmeg, 4 tablespoons parsley, ground black pepper and salt to taste.

Way of preparation:
Divide the cauliflower into florets. Put it to boil in water with a pinch of salt for 10 minutes. Then drain it and sprinkle with nutmeg. Arrange a half of the cauliflower in a small tray.

Heat the oil in a deep pan. Cut the onion finely and put it in the pan. Sauté it for 2-3 minutes. Add the Ground Pork, Worcestershire sauce, pepper and salt to taste. Stew the mixture until the mince is broken into pieces. Spread it on the cauliflower in the tray. On the meat arrange the rest of the cauliflower. Between layers, sprinkle with parsley. Dissolve the tomato paste in ½ cup water. Pour over the dish. Cut bacon into very thin strips. Arrange at the top one another. Preheat the oven to 392 F / 200 C. Put the tray in the oven. Bake the dish for 20 minutes. Serve it warm.

Combines with:
Vegetable salads and vegetable soups - without potatoes; to them may be added meat, chicken, ham, mushrooms, olives, prepared according to the recipes of this book.

4.1. LEEKS WITH BROWN RICE IN THE OVEN

Ingredients for 4 servings:
- 5 leeks (only the white part)
- 1 cup brown rice
- 1 small onion
- 2 cloves garlic
- 2 small carrots
- 1 cup tomatoes
- 3 tablespoons vegetable oil

Spices: 1 teaspoon paprika, 2 tablespoons finely chopped parsley, ground black pepper and salt to taste.

Way of preparation:

Cut the leeks into thin strips with a length of about 0.4 in. (1 cm.). Peel the carrots, onion and garlic and chop them finely. Puree the tomatoes.

Heat a frying pan and put oil to warm. Sauté in it the leeks, onions and garlic for 2-3 minutes. Add carrots and red pepper. Stir the mixture for 2-3 minutes and then add the rice. Add 2 cups of hot water, salt and pepper. Leave the meal to cook on low heat 30 minutes. Transfer the dish on a baking tray. Add the tomatoes and parsley, stir gently. Preheat oven to 392 F (200 C). Put the dish to be baked 10 minutes. This dish could be served as warm and cold.

Serve with: Winter Salad with Sesame

4.2. WINTER SALAD WITH SESAME

Ingredients for 4 servings:
- 3 medium carrots
- 1 small head celery (or 1-2 ribs celery)
- 1 white turnip
- 1 small cucumber
- 2 tablespoons olive oil
- 8 olives

Spices: 7 sprigs finely chopped parsley, Juice from ½ lemon, 1 tablespoon roasted sesame, salt and ground black pepper to taste.

Way of preparation:
Peel the carrots, the white turnip and the celery. Wash them and grate. Cut the cucumber thin circles. Put vegetables in a bowl. Add the olive oil, lemon juice and the spices. Mix the salad carefully. Decorate it with olives and sprinkle it with roasted sesame seeds.

5.1. FISH MEATBALLS WITH CARROT PUREE

Ingredients for 4 servings:
For the meatballs: 28 oz. (800 g.) fillets white fish without skin, 1 very finely chopped onion, 1 tablespoon ground walnut, a pinch grated nutmeg, 1 chili pepper finely chopped, ground black pepper and salt to taste.
For the puree: 3 large carrots, 2 cloves garlic, 2 roasted red sweet peppers, the juice of ½ lemon, 2 sprigs fresh coriander, a pinch ground cumin, 2 tablespoons oil, salt to taste.
Spices: 2 tablespoons oil for grilling the meatballs, 4 sprigs parsley for decoration
Way of preparation:
Carefully cut the fish very finely or grind it in a meat mincer. Place it into a deep bowl. Add all the ingredients for the meatballs. Knead the mixture well until smooth. Smear your hands with oil and form 12 or 15 meatballs. (Depending on what size you prefer to have). Heat the tray in the oven preheated to 428 F / 220 C. Smear it with oil and arrange the meatballs. Pour over them with remaining oil. Bake them for 10 minutes on each side.
For the puree: Peel and cut the carrots into small pieces. Pour over with 2 cups of water. Add a pinch of salt. Put them on the stove; let them cook for 20 minutes. Then, drain them and put them in a deep bowl. Add the remaining ingredients and blend the mixture. If the mixture is thick, add a few tablespoons of water in which you have cooked the carrots.
Serve on the bottom of bowl 2-3 tablespoons pureed carrots. On it put 2 or 3 balls for each portion. Decorate the dish with a sprig parsley.

Combines with:
Vegetable salads and vegetable soups - without potatoes; to them may be added fish, seafood, mushrooms, olives, prepared according to the recipes of this book.

6.1. DUCK FILLET ROASTED IN AN OVEN

Ingredients for 4 servings:
- 4 fillets duck - magret with skin

Spices: 1 tablespoon peeled pumpkin seeds, salt and pepper to taste.

For the puree of celery: 1 head celery about 1 lb. (454 g.), 1 teaspoon butter, a pinch ground white pepper, a pinch grated nutmeg, salt to taste.

Way of preparation:
Heat a shallow pan and place the pumpkin seeds to roast for several minutes.

Sprinkle the fillets with salt and ground black pepper to taste. Put them in a dry heated frying pan on skin side down until they are slightly caramelized. Turn round them. Preheat the oven to 356 F / 180 C. Place the duck fillets in the oven on the grill for 10 minutes, if you want a medium roast (or 15-17 minutes for well-done).

For the puree: Peel the celery and wash it with cold water. Cut it in chunks and put it in a saucepan with 2 cups water and a pinch of salt. Cook the celery about 15 minutes until it become soft. Remove it from the pan and then drain. Place it into a bowl and blend with a mixer or in a blender. If necessary add a little water in which the celery was cooked. Add butter, pepper and nutmeg. Stir until a smooth, homogeneous mixture.

Serve the meal as follows: At the bottom of a shallow dish put puree of celery. On it place one duck fillet. Sprinkle with roasted pumpkin seeds.

Combines with:
Vegetable salads and vegetable soups - without potatoes; to them

may be added meat, chicken, mushrooms, olives, prepared according to the recipes of this book.

7.1. VEGETARIAN BORSCHT

Ingredients for 4 servings:
- 1 small red beet
- 1 medium carrot
- 1sweet onion
- 1-2 cloves garlic
- ½ cup russet potato
- ½ cup fresh cabbage
- 1 red or green bell pepper
- 4 cups hot vegetable broth
- 2 tablespoons vegetable oil

Spices: 2 bay leaves, 2 tablespoons finely chopped parsley, ground black pepper and salt to taste, 2 tablespoons wine vinegar.

Way of preparation:

Clean, peel and wash vegetables. Cut into small cubes red beets, carrots, onions, garlic and potatoes. Cut the cabbage and the pepper into small thin strips.

In a large saucepan, heat the oil. Sauté the onion and the garlic over medium heat for 2 minutes. Add the beetroot, carrots and potatoes. Mix well. After 4 minutes add the cabbage, pepper, bay leaf, hot broth and, if necessary pinch of salt. Put the lid on the saucepan and cook the soup 30 minutes on low heat. Add a pinch ground black pepper and parsley. Serve the soup hot. Optionally you could season it with vinegar.

Serve with: *Potato Stew with Garlic and Mushrooms*

7.2. POTATO STEW WITH GARLIC AND MUSHROOMS

Ingredients for 4 servings:
- 22 oz. (624 g.) Russet Potatoes
- 6 oz. (170 g.) White Mushrooms

- 1 large yellow onion
- 2 cloves garlic
- 3 tablespoons vegetable oil

Spices: 2 tablespoons chopped dill, ground black pepper and salt to taste.

Way of preparation:

Cut the mushrooms, onion and garlic slices. Peel the potatoes, wash them and cut them into medium sized pieces. Put the oil in a deep pan to warm. Add the onion and garlic. Saute them for 2 minutes. Add mushrooms, potatoes, pepper and salt to taste. Do not stir the mixture. After 3 minutes, pour over it with 2 cups of hot water. Put a lid and cook the dish over medium heat until the potatoes become tender. Sprinkle the stew with dill. Serve it warm.

8.1. SMOKED BACON WITH BRUSSELS SPROUTS

Ingredients for 4 servings:

- 12 oz. (340 g.) Smoked Bacon
- 21 oz. (600 g.) Brussels Sprouts
- ½ tablespoon tomato paste
- 2 tablespoons vegetable oil

Spices: 2 tablespoons finely chopped parsley, ground black pepper and salt to taste.

Way of preparation:

Clear Brussels sprouts. Remove the outer leaves if necessary.
Heat the oil in a deep pan. Cut the bacon into small pieces and put it to fry. Then add the Brussels Sprouts, stir. Top up with some hot water and leave to cook for 10 minutes. When the liquid has evaporated, add the tomato paste, pepper and salt to taste. Allow to simmer 10 minutes, stirring periodically. Remove the pan from the fire. Sprinkle the dish with parsley. Serve it warm.

Combines with:

Vegetable salads and vegetable soups - without potatoes; to them may be added meat, ham, chicken, mushrooms, olives, prepared according to the recipes of this book.

9.1. STEW OF PORK LIVER WITH LEEKS

Ingredients for 4 servings:

- 21 oz. (600 g.) Pork Liver
- 5 leeks (white part only)
- 3 roma tomatoes (diced)
- ½ tablespoon tomato paste
- 2 tablespoons vegetable oil

Spices: 2 bay leaves, 2 tablespoons finely chopped parsley, salt and ground black pepper to taste.

Way of preparation:

Clean the liver of blood vessels and mucous membranes. Wash it thoroughly with cold water. Dry it and cut it into pieces. Cut the leeks into thin rings. Simmer it on low heat in hot oil. When the leeks soften, add the chopped liver. Stir until the liver starts to change its color. Then, add the tomatoes, tomato paste, bay leaves, pepper and salt to taste. After 8 minutes, sprinkle the dish with parsley and remove from the heat. Serve it warm.

Combines with:

Vegetable salads and vegetable soups - without potatoes; to them may be added meat, ham, chicken, mushrooms, olives, prepared according to the recipes of this book.

10.1. SOUP FROM SALMON HEAD

Ingredients for 4 servings:

- 1 Salmon Head (you can also use part of the fish bone)
- 3 colored mini sweet peppers
- 1 medium carrot
- 1 white onion
- 1 lemon in slices

Spices: 2 tablespoons chopped parsley, 1 tablespoon chopped dill, salt and ground black pepper to taste.

Way of preparation:

Wash thoroughly the salmon head with cold water. Put it into a pot. Pour over it with 4 cups cold water and put it to cook for 15 minutes. Then remove the head with a slotted spoon and let it cool. Debone it, and take the meat. Strain the fish broth. Peel, wash and cut into small cubes peppers, carrot and onion. Add them to the broth. Sprinkle with salt and pepper to taste. Allow the soup to a boil over medium heat 20 minutes. Add the meat from the fish head. Remove pan from heat and add the spices. Serve the soup warm with a slice lemon and fresh vegetable salad.

Combines with:

Vegetable salads and vegetable dishes - without potatoes; to them may be added fish, seafood, mushrooms, olives, prepared according to the recipes of this book.

11.1. TILAPIA FILLET SOUP AND SHRIMPS

Ingredients for 4 servings:
- 9 oz. (255 g.) Tilapia Fillet
- 5 oz. (142 g.) Shrimps
- 1 cup tomato juice
- ½ tablespoon tomato paste
- 1 large yellow onion
- 2 cloves garlic
- 1 tablespoon oil

Spices: 1 teaspoon basil leaves, 1 tablespoon chopped parsley, ground black pepper and salt to taste.

Way of preparation:

Cut the fish into small pieces. Heat the oil in a pan. Fry the chopped onion and garlic for 2 minutes. Add tomato paste and tomato juice. Stir the mixture for 4 minutes and then pour it into the pan. Add 3 cups hot water, ground black pepper and salt and the fish. Cook the soup 5 minutes and add the shrimps. After 10 minutes remove the pan from the fire. Add basil leaves, chopped parsley and serve the soup warm.

Serve with: *Beetroot Salad with Walnuts*

11.2. BEETROOT SALAD WITH WALNUTS

Ingredients for 4 servings:
- 1 lb. (454 g.) red beets
- 1 tablespoon roasted crushed walnuts
- 1 tablespoon wine vinegar
- leeks (white part only)
- tablespoons oil
- teaspoons mustard
- tablespoon lemon juice

Spices: 1 tablespoon finely chopped coriander, ground white pepper and salt to taste.

Way of preparation:
Clean the leeks and chop it finely. Clean, wash and peel the beetroot. Put it in a pot with boiling water and vinegar (thus preserves its red color). Put the lid and cook for 3 minutes. Then drain the beetroot, cool and grate it coarsely. In a separate bowl, mix the mustard, leeks, lemon juice, ground white pepper and salt. Stir the mixture well and add the beetroot. Put it into a deep serving plate. Sprinkle the salad with coriander, walnuts and the oil.

12.1. ONION SOUP WITH BROCHETTES

Ingredients for 4 servings:
- 4 white onions
- 1 tablespoon flour
- 1 teaspoon butter
- ½ cup white wine cold
- 4 cups vegetable broth

Spices: 1 teaspoon red pepper, a pinch of crushed dried thyme, ground pepper and salt to taste.

For brochettes:

¼ French baguette, 1 clove garlic, 1 tablespoon olive oil, a pinch crushed dried basil or oregano, 1 teaspoon balsamic vinegar.

Way of preparation:

For brochettes:

Cut the baguette in slices. Rub them with the clove of garlic. Mix in a bowl the olive oil vinegar and basil. Apply a light coating on the slices with this mixture. Bake them in the oven at 392 F / 200 C, until golden brown. Remove them and leave to cool.

Peel, wash and cut the onion into thin slices. Melt the butter in a suitable saucepan. Put the onions to stew. Stir not to burn. When acquire a brownish color, add the flour and paprika. Stir and add on trickle cold wine, broth, ground black pepper and salt to taste. Allow the soup to cook over medium heat 15 minutes. Then add the thyme. Remove the pan from the fire.

Put at the bottom of bowls for soup 1 bruschetta. Pour over it with hot soup and serve.

Serve with: *Peppers Stuffed with Groats*

12.2. PEPPERS STUFFED WITH GROATS

Ingredients for 4 servings:
- 4 Red and Green Bell Peppers
- 1 ½ cup groats
- 1 leeks (white part only)
- 1 medium carrot
- 3 tablespoons vegetable oil
- 1 tablespoon flour

Spices: 3 tablespoons finely chopped parsley, salt and ground black pepper to taste.

Way of preparation:

Cut the leeks and carrots into small pieces. Heat 1 tablespoon oil in a pan and sauté the leeks in it for 2 minutes. Add carrots and groats, stir the mixture constantly. After 2-3 minutes, add pepper and salt to taste. Pour over the mixture with 1 ½ cup hot water. Leave the mixture on low heat until the groats is tender. Remove the pan from the fire. Allow the mixture to cool. Add parsley. Stir the mixture and fill the peppers with it. Dip the opening of each stuffed pepper in the flour. Arrange them on a baking tray. Pour ½ cup hot water. Sprinkle the peppers with the remaining oil. Put the pan in a preheated oven to 392 F / 200 C. Bake the dish for about 30 minutes. Serve the peppers stuffed with groats warm.

13.1. TURKEY MEAT SOUP WITH FRAGRANT SPICES

Ingredients for 4 servings:
- 1 lb. (454 g.) Turkey Drumstick
- 1 large onion
- 2 large carrots
- 2 mini sweet peppers
- 1 parsnip

Spices: 1-2 cloves, 1-2 bay leaves, 10 peppercorns, lemon juice and salt to taste.

Way of preparation:
Put the drumstick in a deep saucepan. Pour over it with 5 cups water. Pierce in onion cloves and peppercorns. When the water boils, add the carrots, mini sweet peppers and parsnip cut into large pieces and the whole onion. When the meat is tender, add bay leaves and salt to taste. Continue to cook the soup over low heat (at least 1 hour) until the meat is tender wholly. Remove it, debone it and cut it into chunks. Distribute them in serving dishes. Strain broth and pour it each boiled turkey meat portion. Season it with lemon juice and ground black pepper to taste.

This soup can be prepared in a pressure cooker. Put all the ingredients and spices together in a pot to boil 40 minutes. Then strain the broth.

Serve with: Sauerkraut with Cumin

13.2. SAUERKRAUT WITH CUMIN

Ingredients for 4 servings:

- 2 lbs. (907 g.) Chopped Sauerkraut
- 2 tablespoons tomato diced canned
- 4 tablespoons vegetable oil

Spices: 1 teaspoon ground cumin, 2 teaspoons paprika, 2 tablespoons finely chopped parsley.

Way of preparation:

Heat the oil in a saucepan. Smother the cabbage for 10 minutes, stirring it. Add the paprika and cumin. Pour over it with 1 cup hot water. Stew on low heat until the cabbage is tender. Then add tomatoes, stir. Transfer the meal on a baking tray. Put it into the oven preheated to 392 F / 200 C. Bake the dish until it stays only fat. Serve sprinkled with parsley.

14.1. BEEF LIVER STEW AND PORK MEAT

Ingredients for 4 servings:

- 7 oz. (200 g.)   Beef Liver
- 18 oz. (510 g.) Boneless Pork Stew Meat
- 5 oz. (142 g.) fresh mushrooms
- 2 yellow onions
- ½ cup white wine
- 2 Jalapeno peppers
- 1 tablespoon vegetable oil

Spices: 1 teaspoon paprika, 2 bay leaves, 2 tablespoons finely chopped parsley, ground black pepper and salt to taste.

Way of preparation:

Cut the beef liver on large pieces. Heat the oil in a deep saucepan. Put the meat and stew. Stir until the meat is browned. Then add the sliced onion, coarsely chopped mushrooms, whole chilies and red pepper. Mix well. After 30 minutes, add the liver, bay leaves, ground black pepper and wine. Pour mixture into pan. Preheat the oven to 392 F / 200 C. Put the stew to cook in the oven for 30 minutes. Add salt to taste and serve the stew warm.

Combines with:

Vegetable salads and vegetable soups - without potatoes; to them

may be added meat, chicken, ham, mushrooms, olives, prepared according to the recipes of this book.

15.1. ROASTED PORK TROTTERS

Ingredients for 4 servings:
- 4 Pork Trotters
- 1 large onion
- ½ cup white wine
- 1 tablespoon oil

Spices: 1 cloves, 10 peppercorns, 1 teaspoon red pepper, salt to taste.

Way of preparation:
Peel the onion and cut into quarters. Wash and clean the pork trotters very well. Pour over them with cold water and put them to boil. Separate the foam with a slotted spoon. After 30 minutes, add black pepper, cloves, onion and salt to taste. When the pork trotters are fully cooked, remove them from the pan and debone them. If you have a pressure cooker can use it to boil the pork trotters faster. Arrange the separated meat in a pan greased with oil. Pour over it with wine and sprinkle it with paprika. Preheat the oven to 392 F / 200 C. Bake the meat until golden brown. Serve the roast warm.

<u>**Combines with:**</u>
Vegetable salads and vegetable soups - without potatoes; to them may be added meat, chicken, ham, mushrooms, olives, mustard, prepared according to the recipes of this book.

16.1. MARINATED ROASTED RABBIT MEAT

Ingredients for 4 servings:
- 2 lbs. (907 g.) Rabbit Meat
- 2 tablespoons vegetable oil
- Salt to taste
- 1 Fresh Iceberg Lettuce

For the marinade: 6 cloves garlic, 2 small onions, 4 stalks of parsley, 1 sprig of rosemary, 3 thyme sprigs, 2 twigs oregano, 2 jalapeno peppers, 1/3 cup vinegar, 1 tablespoon paprika, a pinch ground cayenne pepper, 2 bay leaves, 1 cup vegetable broth.

Way of preparation:

Cut the rabbit meat in portions. Cut the onion in slices and the garlic finely. Put them in a deep dish. Add the remaining ingredients for the marinade. Stir them and add the pieces of meat. Cover the container with household foil. Leave it 24 hours in the refrigerator. Then remove the marinated meat and dry it with kitchen paper. Heat the oil in large skillet. Fry the pieces of meat on all sides until golden brown. Transfer them in the tray. Strain the marinade and pour over with it the meat. Sprinkle it with salt to taste. Cover the tray with a lid or aluminum foil. Preheat the oven to 392 F / 200 C. Place the tray in the oven. Bake the dish for 40 minutes. Remove it, discard the foil. Serve each piece of rabbit meat with sauce and fresh Iceberg Lettuce.

Combines with:

Vegetable salads and vegetable soups - without potatoes; to them may be added meat, chicken, ham, mushrooms, olives, mustard, prepared according to the recipes of this book.

17.1. STEWED CHICKEN BREAST WITH SAUSAGE

Ingredients for 4 servings:
- 1 lb. (454 g.) Boneless Chicken Breasts
- 11 oz. (312 g.) Italian Sausage
- 1 large onion
- 5 fresh medium mushrooms
- ½ cup canned tomatoes
- ½ cup white wine
- 2 tablespoons vegetable oil

Spices: 1 teaspoon red pepper, a pinch thyme, ground pepper and salt to taste.

Way of preparation:

Cut the chicken breasts into bite sized pieces, raw sausage into thick wheels, the onion finely, the mushrooms in slices. Heat a deep pan. Place the oil to warm. Place the chicken bites. After 3-4 minutes, add the sausages. Stew them another 3 minutes. Mix them not to burn. Then, remove them with a slotted spoon and put them in a deep dish. In the same fat, saute the onion, mushrooms and tomatoes. After 6 minutes, add them to the chicken and sausages. Add thyme, paprika, salt and pepper to taste. Mix well. Pour the wine. Stew the meal on low heat. The dish must remain only on fat. Serve it warm.

Combines with:

Vegetable salads and vegetable soups - without potatoes; to them may be added meat, chicken, ham, mushrooms, olives, mustard, prepared according to the recipes of this book.

18.1. HALIBUT STEW WITH LEEKS

Ingredients for 4 servings:
- 28 oz. (800 g.) Halibut fillets
- 2 leeks (white part only)
- 1 yellow onion
- 3 cloves garlic
- 14.5 oz. (411 g.) - 1 can petite diced tomatoes
- ½ tablespoon tomato paste
- 2 tablespoons olive oil
- 1 cup hot vegetable or fish broth
- ½ cup white wine

Spices: 15 fresh basil leaves (or fresh cilantro), 2 tablespoons chopped parsley, ground black pepper and salt to taste.

Way of preparation:

Cut the fish fillet into pieces of 1.5 in. – 2 in. (4 - 5 cm.). Heat the olive oil in a deep saucepan over medium heat. Cut the onion and the garlic very finely and leeks into rings. Place the vegetables in the pan to smother for 3 minutes. Add the tomato puree, salt, pepper and the wine. After 3 minutes, add the hot broth, the fish and tomatoes. Stir and cook for 15 minutes. Remove the pan from the heat. Add basil (or cilantro) and parsley. Serve the stew warm.

Combines with:

Vegetable salads and vegetable soups - without potatoes; to them may be added fish, seafood, mushrooms, olives, prepared according to the recipes of this book.

19.1. STUFFED CALAMARI WITH GARNISH

Ingredients for 4 servings:
- 4 large cleaned calamari (tubes only)
- 1 tablespoon olive oil
- 4 skewers or toothpicks

For the filling: 1 tablespoon olive oil, grated ginger root as a small walnut, 2 finely chopped onions, 2 cloves finely chopped garlic 2 tablespoon finely chopped parsley, ground black pepper and salt to taste, a pinch crushed red pepper.

Way of preparation:

Wash the calamari (tubes) thoroughly with cold water. Dry them well with kitchen paper. Thus, the tubes are ready for filling.

For the filling: Heat oil in a pan. Fry the ginger in it for 30 seconds and add the onions. Stir the mixture and leave it on the fire until the onion softens. Add the garlic and let the entire mixture to stew for 5 minutes. Then add salt and pepper, crushed red pepper, parsley. Stir the mixture well and let it cool. Put in calamari (tubes) a little of the ready filling. (Do not overfill) Close the openings with skewer or toothpick. Preheat grill pan (or grill). Grease the bottom with olive oil. Place the stuffed calamari to be roasted for 3 minutes on each side, turning round them occasionally. Remove the calamari and distribute them to serving dishes. For garnish add fresh vegetables (Fresh Blend Salads or Cucumbers with Green Onions).

This dish must be served hot immediately after its preparation. The calamari when cool are not tasty because they are stringy.

Combines with:

Vegetable salads and vegetable soups - without potatoes; to them may be added fish, seafood, mushrooms, olives, prepared according to the recipes of this book.

20.1. TURKEY STUFFED WITH CHICKEN AND CHESTNUTS

Products for 1 Turkey (around 16-18 servings):
- 1 small turkey about 13 ½ lbs. (6.000 g.)
- lb. (454 lb.) peeled chestnuts
- 7 oz. (200 g.) chicken minced meat
- 1 large onion (diced)
- 1 cup vegetable broth
- tablespoons butter

Spices: ground black pepper and salt to taste.

Way of preparation:

Clean and wash the turkey. Salt it inside and out and then rub with pepper. Boil the peeled and cleaned from skin chestnuts in water with salt to taste. Then cut them into very small pieces or grind them. Stew the minced chicken meat and the onion in a little butter. Add the chestnuts and mix. Fill the turkey with this mixture. Sew it with a strong thread. Place it into a suitable deep tray with a lid. If you do not have a lid use aluminum foil. Pour over the turkey with remaining oil. Preheat the oven to 338 F / 170 C. Place the turkey to bake in the oven between 4 hours. Once browned on all sides, add broth and cover it up. From time to time pour over it with the sauce, in which it is baked. Serve each portion of turkey meat with part of the filling.

Combines with:

Vegetable salads and vegetable soups - without potatoes; to them may be added chicken, meat, ham, mushrooms, olives, mustard, prepared according to the recipes of this book.

WINTER - DINNER

21.1. BAKED WHOLE TROUT IN FOIL

Ingredients for 4 servings:
- 4 Trout - small (whole)
- 6 oz. (170 g.) shallots, cut short
- 2 tablespoons olive oil
- 1 tablespoon tomato paste

Spices: 8 dill sprigs, 8 thin slices lemon, 1 clove pressed garlic, ground black pepper, 1 teaspoon sea salt, foil or baking paper.

Way of preparation:

The trout must be cleaned and well washed with cold water. Dry it. Rub its skin with garlic. Sprinkle it from inside and outside with pepper, sea salt and olive oil. Smear outside the whole fish with tomato paste. Put in the belly of each fish 2 slices of lemon, 2 dill sprigs and shallots. Prepare a large enough piece of foil. Smear it with olive oil. Place the fish in the middle. Wrap the foil around the fish as the top leave a small opening. Preheat the oven to 428 F / 220 C. Place the foil packet on the grill or in the oven on a tray near the grill. Bake the trout for 25 minutes. Serve the fish on the foil in a wide shallow dinner plate. Before serving, expand the opening. Add fresh salad.

Combines with:

Vegetable salads and vegetable soups - without potatoes; to them may be added fish, seafood, mushrooms, olives, prepared according to the recipes of this book.

22.1. POTATO ROLL WITH VEGETABLES

Ingredients for 4 servings:
- 2 lbs. (907 g.) Russet Potatoes
- 2 medium carrots
- ½ cup celery
- 2 pickled cucumbers
- 1 cup fresh or marinated mushroom

- 1 teaspoon butter

Spices: 2 tablespoons finely chopped parsley, 1 teaspoon oregano or savory, ground black pepper and salt to taste.

Way of preparation:

Peel the potatoes, carrots and celery. Wash them and cut them into pieces. Put them in a saucepan with 5 cups of water and 1 teaspoon salt. Put the pan over medium heat. When the vegetables become tender, drain them of water and blend them. Add the chopped mushrooms and cucumbers. Stir the mixture well and add pepper, parsley, oregano or savory and ½ teaspoon butter. Knead the mixture and shape of it a roll. Put it in a greased pan. Apply the roll with remaining butter. Preheat the oven to 392 F / 200 C. Put the tray in the oven. The roll must be baked for about 25 minutes. Serve it warm with fresh salad.

Serve with: Red Beet Salad with Spicy Dressing

22.2. RED BEET SALAD WITH SPICY DRESSING

Ingredients for 4 servings:

- 1 lb. (454 g.) Red Beet

For the dressing: 1 tablespoon Dijon mustard, 3 tablespoons lemon juice, 3 tablespoons olive oil, 1 leek (white part only), salt and ground black pepper to taste.

Way of preparation:

Peel the beet and wash it with cold water. Cut it into thin slices and arrange on serving plates.

For the dressing: Mix in a bowl the mustard, lemon juice, salt and pepper. Add on trickle of olive oil and 1-2 tablespoons of hot water. Add the leeks cut into very small pieces. Stir the mixture well. Pour over each portion beets with a little dressing. This salad can be served the next day.

23.1. PORK LOIN BABYBACK RIBS IN IRISH

Ingredients for 4 servings:

- 4 lbs. (1.814 g.) Pork Loin Babyback Ribs
- 1 cup of dark beer
- 1 tablespoon vegetable oil

Spices: a pinch of chili, 1 teaspoon paprika, 1 teaspoon ground black pepper .

Way of preparation:

Coat the bottom of medium tray oil. Cut the ribs in portions. Rub them well with the spices. Arrange ribs in the tray. Carefully pour the beer into the tray. Allow the ribs to stand for 2 hours. Cover the tray with aluminum foil. Preheat the oven to 392 F / 200 C. Put the tray with the ribs in the oven for 1 ½ hours. Then remove foil and bake for at least 20 minutes until ribs become golden brown. Serve them with mustard and salad of marinated sweet onions.

Serve with: *Marinated Sweet Onion Salad*

23.2. MARINATED SWEET ONION SALAD

Ingredients for 4 servings:

- 4 large sweet onions

For the marinade: a bay leaf, 1 clove, 5 peppercorns, salt to taste, 3 tablespoons wine vinegar.

Spices: 2 tablespoons olive oil, a pinch of cinnamon, 2 tablespoons finely chopped parsley.

Way of preparation:

Bring to a boil 4 cups of water along with the bay leaf, cloves, black pepper and salt to taste. Cut the onion into slices. Put it in a pot and pour over with the hot marinade. Cook it for 2 minutes. Remove the container from the heat and add the vinegar in it. Allow the onions to stand in this mixture for 1 hour. Then drain well and sprinkle with olive oil, cinnamon and parsley.

24.1. BEEF STEWED WITH SPICES

Ingredients for 4 servings:

- 25 oz. (708 g.) Boneless Beef
- 1 medium carrot
- 1 sweet onion
- 2 ribs celery
- 2 tablespoons oil
- ½ cup white wine
- 2 cups beef broth
- 5 sprigs of parsley

Spices: 2 cloves garlic, 1 clove, the zest of 1 lemon, 2 tablespoons finely chopped parsley, 1 tablespoon finely chopped celery leaves, ground black pepper and salt to taste

Way of preparation:

Cut into small pieces carrot, onion and celery. Put them at the bottom of a deep pan with oil and parsley stalks. Place the whole piece of meat over the vegetables. Put the lid on the saucepan. When the meat starts change its color, add garlic, clove, lemon zest, wine and 2 cups of beef broth (or hot water). Allow the meat to stew over low heat. When the meat is soft enough, remove it from the pan and leave it for 15 minutes to "rest". Then cut it into thin slices.

Strain the broth. Add salt to taste, black pepper, finely chopped parsley and celery leaves. Serve each portion of meat with hot sauce and salad of black turnip.

<u>**Serve with:**</u> *Salad of Black Turnip and Carrots*

24.2. SALAD OF BLACK TURNIP AND CARROTS

Ingredients for 4 servings:
- 14 oz. (400 g.) Black Turnip
- 2 large carrots
- 1 small sweet onion
- 2 tablespoons vegetable oil

Spices: 2 tablespoons finely chopped parsley, ground black pepper and salt to taste.

Way of preparation:

Peel and grate the carrots coarsely on grater. Cut the onions into small cubes. Peel the turnip and then grate on a grater. Wash it several times in cold water and wring it out well. Then mix it with carrots, onions and parsley. Salt the salad to taste and put it in a serving plate. Pour over it with oil. Sprinkle it with pepper to taste.

25.1. STEWED CAULIFLOWER WITH SAUCE

Ingredients for 4 servings:
- 1 Fresh Head Cauliflower – medium
- 1 teaspoon butter
- 2 tablespoons flour
- 2 cups vegetable broth
- 2 tablespoons crushed walnuts
- Toasted whole-grain bread

Spices: 2 tablespoons finely chopped parsley, a pinch of ground cumin, a pinch of grated nutmeg, salt and ground black pepper to taste.

Way of preparation:
Clean the cauliflower and tear it into florets. Wash it with cold water. Put it in a pot, add salt to taste and 4 cups of hot water. Stew the cauliflower over medium heat until soft (about 8 minutes). Drain it.

Heat the butter in a suitable frying pan and add the flour. Stir constantly to avoid burn. When it acquires yellow color pour on a thin stream 2 cups of broth. When the sauce thickens enough, add the cauliflower and the spices. Allow the meal on fire another 1-2 minutes. Add walnuts and stir. Serve warm with toast bread.

Instead of vegetable broth, you can use the broth of boiling the cauliflower.

Combines with:
Vegetable salads and vegetable soups - without potatoes; to them may be added croutons, spaghetti, pasta, bread crumbs, flour, bread, mushrooms, olives (prepared according to the recipes of

this book).

26.1. CHICKEN WINGS WITH CRUNCHY CRUST

Ingredients for 4 servings:
- 3 lbs. (1.360 g.) Chicken Wings

Spices: 4 tablespoons lemon juice, 2 tablespoons vegetable oil, 2 teaspoons paprika, ground pepper and salt to taste.

Way of preparation:
Wash the chicken wings thoroughly with cold water. Drain them and dry them with kitchen paper. Put them in a deep baking tray. Sprinkle them with all the spices. Stir them with the hands, so to take the entire quantity of spices. Let them to stay until the oven will be heated to 392 F / 200 C. Pour into the tray 1 coffee cup of water. Then, place it in the oven at a moderate level. Bake the wings 40 minutes, until golden brown well. Serve them warm.

<u>Combines with:</u>
Vegetable salads and vegetable soups - without potatoes; to them may be added chicken, meat, ham, mushrooms, olives, mustard (prepared according to the recipes of this book).

27.1. BEEF BRISKET WITH ROSEMARY

Ingredients for 4 servings:
- 28 oz. (800 g.) Boneless Beef Brisket - whole piece
- 8 sprigs fresh rosemary

Spices: 4 cloves garlic, ground pepper to taste.

For the sauce: 1 cup red wine, salt and ground black pepper to taste, the resulting sauce of roasted, ½ cup beef broth.

Way of preparation:
Leave the piece of the Beef Brisket outside the refrigerator for one hour. Preheat the oven to 320 F / 160 C. Rub the meat well with one or two cloves of garlic and a pinch of ground black pepper. On the grate of the baking pan arrange the washed and well dried

stalks of rosemary, the remaining garlic cloves halved in two. On them place the meat - fat side up. Put in the tray 1 cup of water and put the meat to bake in the oven. When the meat is well browned and is almost ready, take a little bit of the separated on the bottom juices and pour it gently. Close the oven door. Meat will be well cooked after about 4 hours. Watch it to bake according to your taste. Once the meat is ready, remove it from the oven and leave it to "rest" for 15 minutes. Cut it into thin slices before serving.

For the sauce: Take a spoon most of the fat from the resulting the juice of the baking. Place the pan over low heat. Scrape the caramelized parts of the sides and bottom of the tray. Then add the wine, broth, salt and ground black pepper to taste. Stir until the sauce thickens.

Serve each portion of Beef Brisket roast (2 slices) and pour over them with a little hot sauce.

Garnish it with fresh vegetable salad.

Combines with:

Vegetable salads and vegetable soups - without potatoes; to them may be added meat, ham, chicken, mushrooms, olives, mustard (prepared according to the recipes of this book).

28.1. CELERY WITH GARLIC SAUCE

Ingredients for 4 servings:
- 2 medium heads of celery
- 3 tablespoons olive oil
- 1 tablespoon crushed walnuts

Spices: salt and ground black pepper to taste.

For the garlic sauce: 1 ½ cups yogurt, 2 cloves pressed garlic, 2 tablespoons chopped dill, salt.

Way of preparation:

Peel, wash and cut the heads of celery on halves. Then each one cut into thin slices. Put them in a bowl. Sprinkle them with salt and pepper. Pour over them with olive oil and mix them. Heat a grill pan. Arrange the slices of celery. Bake them on each side for 5 minutes over medium heat.

Prepare garlic sauce in a separate bowl. Mix 1 ½ cups yogurt, 2 cloves pressed garlic, 2 tablespoons chopped dill, salt to taste and mix them.

Serve each bowl by few slices of cooked celery. Add 2 tablespoons of garlic sauce. Sprinkle them with crushed walnuts. This dish is delicious also when is chilled.

Serve with: *Chicory Salad with Cheese*

28.2. CHICORY SALAD WITH CHEESE

Ingredients for 4 servings:
- 2 Fresh White Chicory
- 5 oz. (142 g.) cheese of your choice
- 2 ribs celery
- 1 tablespoon roasted crushed walnuts

For the dressing: 2 tablespoons olive oil, 1-2 tablespoons vinegar, ½ tablespoon "Dijon" mustard.

Spices: salt and ground black pepper to taste, 2 tablespoons finely chopped parsley.

Way of preparation:

Prepare the dressing. Put all ingredients in a bowl and stir them vigorously.

Clean and wash the leaves of chicory. Dry them and put them in a wide serving plate. Peel, wash and chop the celery finely. Cut the small cube cheese. Evenly distribute the celery, walnuts and cheese on chicory. Sprinkle the salad with the ground black pepper, dressing and parsley. Optionally you can add a little salt.

29.1. JELLY BEEF TONGUE

Ingredients for 4 servings:
- 26 oz. (737 g.) Beef Tongue
- 2 small pickled cucumbers

- 1 large carrot
- 1 tablespoon mustard
- 1 tablespoon soft butter
- ½ oz. (15 g.) unflavored gelatin
- 20 leaves of parsley
- 1 tablespoon finely chopped parsley
- salt to taste

Spices: 2 bay leaves, cardamom, 10 grains pepper.

Way of preparation:

Place the tongue whole in a pressure cooker with cold water and spices. Once the water boils, cook the tongue for 1 hour. Then, drain it well and peel while warm. Cut it into small cubes. Mix them with mustard and butter. Stir them well. Add chopped diced cucumbers, carrots, and finally the tongue. Sprinkle with salt to taste. Stir gently.

Mix the gelatin with a little tepid water. After 15 minutes, add to it 1 cup hot broth in which you have boiled the tongue. Stir the mixture well and let it cool down.

Decorate with leaves of parsley the edge of the bowls in which the tongue will be gelatinized. Distribute them in a mixture of vegetables and tongue. Pour over them with tepid gelatin and put them to stand in a refrigerator for several hours. Before serving the jellied tongue, dip bowls in hot water and turn on shallow dishes. Sprinkle each serving with chopped parsley.

Combines with:

Vegetable salads and vegetable soups - without potatoes; to them may be added meat, ham, chicken, mushrooms, olives, mustard, prepared according to the recipes of this book.

30.1. STUFFED CHICKEN

Ingredients for 4 servings:

- 1 small chicken
- 5 oz. (142 g.) ground pork meat
- 1 small onion

- 1 red sweet pepper
- 2 pickled cucumbers
- 4 oz. (113 g.) fresh mushrooms
- 3 tablespoons oil

Spices: 2 tablespoons lemon juice, 1 tablespoon chopped parsley, 1 tablespoon basil, ground pepper and salt to taste.

Way of preparation:

Debone the raw chicken, trying chicken to remain whole. Apply it inside and out with lemon juice and pepper. Let it stand in the refrigerator for 2 hours. Cut the onion, red sweet pepper and mushrooms into small pieces. Heat 2 tablespoon oil and sauté in it the onion, red sweet pepper, mushrooms and minced meat. Finally add the cucumbers cut into small cubes, parsley, basil and salt to taste. Fill the chicken with this mixture. Sew the chicken with a strong thread. Coat the chicken with the oil. Put it in a small tray. Pour in ½ glass of water first. Preheat the oven to 392 F / 200 C. Place the tray with the chicken. Bake it for 1 hour. During baking pour the chicken with its own sauce. Serve the whole chicken on a board. Cut it in slices and serve warm with fresh vegetable salad.

<u>**Combines with:**</u>

Vegetable salads and vegetable soups - without potatoes; to them may be added meat, ham, chicken, mushrooms, olives, mustard (prepared according to the recipes of this book).

31.1. ORIGINAL FISH SOUP WITH BROCCOLI

Ingredients for 4 servings:
- 14 oz. (400 g.) Cod Fillets without skin
- 7 oz. (200 g.) fresh cut Broccoli Crowns
- 1 small parsnip root
- 1 small parsley root
- 1 small carrot
- 2 ribs celery
- 1 yellow onion

- 1 tablespoon olive oil

Spices: 10-12 chopped peppermint leaves, 6 coriander leaves, 2 tablespoons lemon juice, ground black pepper and salt to taste.

Way of preparation:

Cut the Cod Fillets on portions.

Peel, wash and cut the vegetables on coarsely. Sauté them in a pan with hot oil for 2-3 minutes. Pour over them with 4 cups of hot water, add salt to taste. Cook them for 20 minutes. Strain the broth, remove the vegetables. Return the soup to the pot.

Sprinkle cut broccoli crowns with black pepper and put them in vegetable broth. Add the fish. Cook the soup for 10 minutes. Remove the pan from the fire. Put the spices and serve while it is hot.

Combines with:

Vegetable salads and vegetable dishes - without potatoes; to them may be added fish, seafood, mushrooms, olives (prepared according to the recipes of this book).

32.1. STEW POTATOES WITH LEEKS

Ingredients for 4 servings:

- 2 lbs. (907 g.) Russet Potatoes
- 4 leeks (only the white part)
- 1 yellow onion
- 3 tablespoons oil

Spices: 1 teaspoon paprika, 1 teaspoon savory (or oregano), 2 tablespoons finely chopped parsley, salt and ground black pepper to taste.

Way of preparation:

Clean the leeks and onion, cut them into thin rings. Peel the potatoes and cut them into large cubes. Heat the oil in a saucepan. Sauté the leeks and onion in it for 3 minutes. Add potatoes and paprika. Stir and pour over the mixture with 2 cups hot water. Add pepper and salt to taste. Leave the meal to simmer until potatoes become tender. Add parsley and savory (oregano).

Remove the pan from the fire. Serve hot with vegetable salad.
Combines with:
Vegetable salads and vegetable soups - to them may be added potatoes, mushrooms, olives (prepared according to the recipes of this book).

33.1. KEBAB OF BEEF WITH RED WINE

Ingredients for 4 servings:
- 1 lb. 10 oz. (737 g.) Boneless Beef Stew Meat
- 2 yellow onions
- ½ cup red wine
- 3 tablespoons vegetable oil
- 5 cloves garlic

Spices: 1 teaspoon paprika, 2 bay leaves, 10 peppercorns, 1 tablespoon chopped parsley, ground black pepper and salt to taste.

Way of preparation:
Clean and chop the onion on slices. Sprinkle the meat with ground black pepper and salt. Put it to stew with the oil. Stir for 3 minutes and then add the onions and cloves garlic. After 5 minutes add the paprika. Pour over the mixture with wine and 1 cup hot water. Let the meat to simmer on low heat. When the meat is tender (after about 90 minutes), add the bay leaves and peppercorns. Increase the heat and let the dish to simmer for additional 10 minutes.
Serve the dish warm with fresh vegetable salad. Sprinkle it with chopped parsley.

Combines with:
Vegetable salads and vegetable soups - without potatoes; to them may be added meat, ham, chicken, mushrooms, olives, mustard (prepared according to the recipes of this book).

34.1. SKEWERS WITH PORK AND BACON

Ingredients for 4 servings:
- 1 lb. 8 oz. (680 g.) Boneless Pork Loin
- 1 white onion
- 6 oz. (170 g.) Bacon
- 2 tablespoons vegetable oil
- ½ lemon

Spices: juice of 1 lemon, ground black pepper and salt to taste.
Way of preparation:
Cut the bacon into very thin strips.
Cut the onion very finely. Cut the meat into thin slices with a width of 1.25 in (3 cm.). Hammer them and sprinkle with black pepper, lemon, onion and oil. Leave to stand for 3 hours in the refrigerator (maybe longer). Then drain them, wrap them into small rolls-bites. Wrap each roll-bite with bacon strips.
Thread on skewers by 3 - 4 rolls. Preheat grill pan. Smear it with oil and place the skewers to bake. Turn them from time to time. Serve hot with a slice of lemon and salad.
Serve with: Iceberg Lettuce Salad with Bacon

34.2. ICEBERG LETTUCE SALAD WITH BACON

Ingredients for 4 servings:
- 1 Fresh Iceberg Lettuce
- 4 radishes
- 4 oz. (113 g.) Bacon into thin strips
- 1 small red onion
- 8 olives

Spices: salt to taste, 2 tablespoons lemon juice, 4 slices of lemon.
Way of preparation:
Wash the salad thoroughly with cold water. Dry it Shred the leaves into pieces and put them in a bowl. Cut the radishes into slices and add them. Cut the onion into thin slices and put it in the bowl. Stir the vegetables. Put the bacon on them. Sprinkle the salad with salt and lemon. Decorate it with olives and lemon

slices.

35.1. TURKEY BREASTS WITH CAULIFLOWER

Ingredients for 4 servings:
- 1 lb. 2 oz. (510 g.) Boneless Turkey Breasts
- 12 oz. (340 g.) fresh cauliflower
- 2 leeks
- 2 cloves garlic
- 2 mini sweet peppers
- ½ tablespoon tomato paste
- ½ cup white wine
- 1 cup vegetable broth
- 2 tablespoon oil

Spices: 1 teaspoon thyme, grated nutmeg, ground black pepper and salt to taste.

Way of preparation:

Wash the cauliflower and tear it into florets. Put it in a deep pan and pour over with water. Add a pinch of salt. Allow to boil for 10 minutes. Then drain. Cut the leeks, peppers and garlic into thin strips. Sprinkle the turkey breasts with ground black pepper and salt. Heat the pan and put in it the oil. When it gets warm - put the turkey breast to cook for 7 minutes on each side. Add the leeks, peppers, garlic and wine. Add the tomato paste after 2 minutes. Stir and put cauliflower, vegetable broth and nutmeg. Cook the meal, until thickened. Sprinkle it with thyme. Serve it warm.

Combines with:

Vegetable salads and vegetable soups - without potatoes; to them may be added chicken, meat, ham, mushrooms, olives, mustard (prepared according to the recipes of this book).

36. 1. WHOLE ROAST CHICKEN IN IRISH

Ingredients for 4 servings:
1 small whole chicken

- 1 teaspoon butter
- ½ cup of dark beer

Spices: 1 teaspoons paprika, ground black pepper and salt to taste.

Way of preparation:

Dry the chicken. Rub it from outside and inside with pepper and salt. Mix the butter with paprika. Smear the chicken with this mixture thoroughly. Put it in a fireproof container. Pour over it with beer. Cover the pot with a lid or aluminum foil. Preheat the oven to 392 F / 200 C. Place the chicken to be baked for 1 hour. Remove the cover (foil) and bake the chicken for another 10 minutes. Divide the ready chicken into portions. Pour over each portion with sauce from the baking. Serve the roasted chicken warm and vegetable salad.

Combines with:

Vegetable salads and vegetable soups - without potatoes; to them may be added chicken, meat, ham, mushrooms, olives, mustard (prepared according to the recipes of this book).

37.1. ICELANDIC COD LOIN WITH ONION AND OLIVES

Ingredients for 4 servings:

- 1 lb. 6 oz. (624 g.) Fresh Icelandic Cod Loin
- 3 white onions
- 8 pitted olives
- 1 tablespoon crushed walnuts
- 1 tablespoon capers
- 1 tablespoon olive oil
- 2 tablespoons lemon juice

Spices: ground black pepper and salt to taste, 8 sliced lemon.

Way of preparation:

Cut the onion into slices. Heat olive oil in a pan. Sauté the onion for 3 minutes. Pour it into baking tray. Salt the fish fillets sprinkle them with pepper. Arrange them on stewed onions. Sprinkle with lemon juice. Add the olives and capers around the fish fillets. Sprinkle the meal with walnuts. Preheat the oven to 428 F / 220

C. Put the fish to bake 20 minutes. Thus prepared fish fillet is delicious when it is warm. Serve each portion with a slice of lemon and fresh vegetable salad.

Combines with:

Vegetable salads and vegetable soups - without potatoes; to them may be added fish, seafood, mushrooms, olives (prepared according to the recipes of this book).

38.1. SHRIMPS WITH TOMATO SAUCE

Ingredients for 4 servings:
- 1 lb. 2 oz. (510 g.) Raw Large Shrimps
- 1 ½ cups peeled canned tomatoes
- 2 cloves garlic
- 1 sweet onion
- 1 tablespoon olive oil
- ½ cup white wine

Spices: 2 fresh twigs of thyme, 2 tablespoons finely chopped parsley, ground black pepper and salt to taste.

Way of preparation:

Chop finely the onion, garlic and tomatoes. Clean the shrimps and wash them thoroughly with cold water. Put on the stove to heat a deep pan. Pour the olive oil and add the onions and garlic. Stir and allow sautéing for 2 minutes. Add wine, tomatoes, thyme, salt and pepper to taste. Leave the sauce to simmer on low heat 10 minutes. Preheat the oven to 374 F / 190 C. Place the shrimps in a baking tray. Pour over them with the sauce. Sprinkle the dish with parsley. Put the tray in the oven. Allow to cook for 15 minutes. Serve the dish warm.

Combines with:

Vegetable salads and vegetable soups - without potatoes; to them may be added fish, seafood, mushrooms, olives (prepared according to the recipes of this book).

39.1. BBQ-FISH SKEWERS WITH ONION AND LEMON

Ingredients for 4 servings:
- 1 lb. 5 oz. (600 g.) Salmon Fillet - skinless
- 2 sweet onions
- 2 lemons
- 1 tablespoon olive oil

Spices: ground black pepper and salt to taste, the juice of ½ lemon.

Way of preparation:
For this recipe you can use wood, bamboo or metal skewers small. Cut the fish fillets into pieces by 0.8 in (2 cm.) for skewers. Cut the onion into chunks, lemons on 8 pieces. Sprinkle the fish with the onion and pepper and salt to taste. Thread on skewers at a small distance from each other a piece of fish, a piece of onion, a piece of fish, a slice of lemon, a piece of fish. Sprinkle the fish skewers with olive oil and lemon juice. Warm up on medium heat the grill or a grill pan. Place the skewers on the grill (grill pan). Leave them to be baked for 6 minutes on each side. Remove them from the grill and place them in a hot dish. Serve the fish skewers warm and fresh vegetable salad.

Combines with:
Vegetable salads and vegetable soups - without potatoes; to them may be added fish, seafood, mushrooms, olives (prepared according to the recipes of this book).

40.1. ROASTED SMALL PIG FOR HOLIDAYS

Ingredients for 10-12 servings:
- 1 little pig about 7 - 8 lb.
- 4 tablespoons vegetable oil
- Vine twigs or grill

Spices: 2 teaspoons paprika, ground black pepper and salt to taste.

Way of preparation:
In a large pan put a wreath of braided vine twigs. On them place

the pig coated with a mixture of oil, ground black pepper and paprika. Preheat the oven to 428 F / 220 C. Put the pig in the tray and roast it about 15 minutes. Then reduce oven to 302 F / 150 C).

Bake the pig a few hours, occasionally brushing it with oil for crispy rind. Salt the roasted pig and serve it whole.

Combines with:

Vegetable salads and vegetable soups - without potatoes; to them may be added chicken, meat, ham, mushrooms, olives, mustard (prepared according to the recipes of this book).

Made in United States
Troutdale, OR
07/01/2023

10925424R00139